LEARNING TO FLY IN 21 DAYS

Phil Stone

NEXUS
SPECIAL INTERESTS

NEXUS SPECIAL INTERESTS

Nexus Special Interests Ltd.
Nexus House
Azalea Drive
Swanley
Kent BR8 8HU
England

ISBN 1-85486-212-X

Acknowledgements

I am very grateful to a number of people who helped me in realising my dream of becoming a pilot. First and foremost, for his patience and advice, and indeed his cajoling along the route I must thank my instructor Nic Mostert. Nic had to put up with a lot during my period of training and I hope that he has survived the experience.

By the same token I am extremely grateful to Margaret and Eric Shipley who own the flight school at which I trained, Britannia Flight Centre. The standard of training and the service that they provided can only be described as totally thorough and efficient.

Finally, I must thank Chrissie Alton who not only supported my dream of learning to fly but also actively encouraged me to write this totally unique book. I am also grateful for the countless hours she has spent in reading and correcting my draft manuscripts and indeed, perhaps of more consequence, for having the courage to fly with me as a passenger once I had gained my licence.

Phil Stone

The Author

Phil Stone is a Management Consultant who specialises in assisting businesses with Business Planning and Strategy. Independently accredited by the British Accreditation Bureau most of the work that he undertakes is through the nation-wide network of Business Links and Training and Enterprise Councils.

He is also an accomplished author having written a number of books on a variety of business management subjects together with a guide book for pilots flying in Florida.

Contents

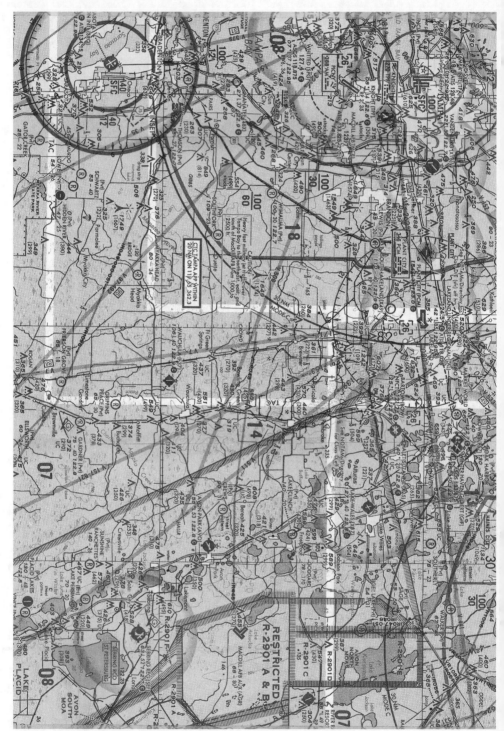

Fig 1. Bartow Airfield Environs

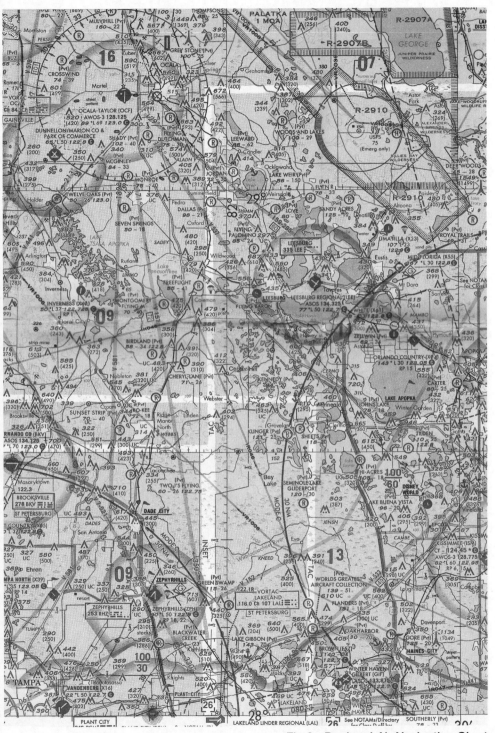

Fig 2. Regional Air Navigation Chart

Learning to Fly in 21 Days

Introduction

This book is not about the technical aspects of learning to fly. It is intended as a practical guide to the physical and emotional aspects of learning to fly and has been written in order to help you try and understand exactly what you are about to undertake and hopefully prepare you for the pain, anguish and despair that you will sometimes feel as well as the elation of achieving the various goals along the route to a Private Pilot's Licence.

It should be noted that at the time of writing the requirements to achieve a Private Pilot's Licence are under significant review and change with the introduction of a standardised system throughout the European Union and whilst the basic flight training will broadly remain the same the written examinations may change. The practical examinations, referred to in this book as the Navigation Flight Test and the General Flight Test have already been the subject of review and have now been combined into the Skill Test. You are therefore encouraged to obtain up-to-date information in this regard from your chosen flight school.

I gained my Private Pilot's Licence on an intensive three-week course in Florida in June 1997 having previously only completed a one-hour trial lesson in the United Kingdom at my local flying school.

Initially it seemed an impossible task associated with a great deal of humiliation and anxiety but it is possible: I was nearly forty years old upon completion, and hopefully this book will go some way to preparing you for the undoubted stress that lies ahead.

Whichever way you choose to gain your Private Pilot's Licence, either by the intensive three or four-week training course or over a period of months, I wish you good luck and safe flying.

Cessna 150 registration N66560 used for the vast majority of the author's training - 45 hours 30 minutes logged in this aircraft out of total training time.

Chapter One

The Preparation

I t all started with a newspaper article in the early part of 1997. The article looked at the various options that aspiring private pilots had with regard to obtaining a Private Pilot's Licence (PPL) and the costs involved.

Having looked at the possibility of gaining a licence some years previously I was surprised at how much the actual cost had diminished in real terms with the cost in the UK being probably in the region of £5,000. The article did however report that an option was available to undertake an intensive three or four-week course in various places throughout the world such as the United States, South Africa, New Zealand and Cyprus, obviously on the basis that the weather would be ideal for most of the year. Quite apart from the weather aspect, the cost appeared to be at least half that of gaining a licence in the UK.

This was an appealing option: living in the North East of England the weather cannot be guaranteed from one day to the next and to undertake the required minimum hours to achieve the licence it could well have taken potentially at least six months. Even then that would be on the basis of flying at least seven hours per month and, at a cost of £600 per month, this seemed to me to be excessive.

Over the next few months I bought most of the available flying magazines, including 'Pilot' and 'Flyer', all of which carried numerous advertisements for flying schools throughout the world. All offered the potential of completing the PPL in three or four weeks and at much the same cost of about £2,000. Having looked at the add-on costs such as commercial flight and living expenses I decided that Florida was my best option.

The next stage in my plan was to select a flight school from the variety of advertisements that were in each magazine and so followed a number of faxes to these schools asking for details of the course, the accommodation, if any, that was offered as part of the cost, the school's pass rates and references from former students. To me, the last question was the most important. Reputation is everything in all service industries and unless the selected school could satisfy me on that point then they would not gain my business.

Within hours of sending off a number of faxes I was amazed to get a response from one school by way of a personal telephone call offering me all the information that I required, together with two local references in the North East of England both of whom had completed their licences in the previous months. Following on from the telephone call I received a three-page fax giving me specific details of the syllabus and the training that was offered. It also gave me the assurance that my instructor would remain the same throughout the course. Not having considered this aspect previously, it struck me that provided I got on personally with him or her, this would be a major benefit. It would remove the obvious drawback of having to go over old ground with each instructor so that he or she could assess my progress. To say that I was impressed with the speed and quality of the response I received from this first school would be an understatement. But, bearing in mind the amount of money involved I was not going to go with this first school without details from any of the other potential schools that I had initially shortlisted.

As it transpired, first impressions counted a lot in this case and having spoken to the two references, both of whom offered excellent reports, and having considered the information that had arrived from other schools, I eventually decided that this school would be the one. There were, however, two other important elements to consider before booking my place on the course and my flight ticket to Florida. The first was the question of whether I would actually like being in a small aircraft. All very well to look and admire them from a distance whilst dreaming of being a pilot, but what would I feel like once actually up in the air? It would be no good to suffer from airsickness having already incurred the expense. The second concern was my health. Despite being considered an average, healthy individual I had no idea of the actual physical requirements for the medical certificate I would require enabling me to fly in the UK. There would be little point in incurring the expense of gaining the licence unless I could satisfy the requirements of the medical. This therefore left me with two things to do before committing myself fully. I needed to book a trial flight with the Newcastle Aero Club and book an appointment to see the Civil Aviation Authority Medical Examiner in order to get a medical certificate.

The day of the trial flight dawned and I duly reported to the Aero Club at the appointed time to meet the instructor and establish in my own mind whether I could indeed enjoy the pleasures of flying a light aircraft. I was introduced to the instructor and taken out to the aircraft, a Piper Cadet, G-BRJV. I was shown around and had the basic exterior components of the aircraft explained to me in terms of what they did and what effect they would have once in the air, in addition to checking that all was well with the aircraft prior to the flight. With the benefit of hindsight I should perhaps have read beforehand 'Trial Flight Guide' written by David Bruford which explains exactly what to expect on the first flight and this may be something that you should consider before taking your first lesson.

In then to the cockpit. It was somewhat of a surprise to be placed in the left-hand seat as I knew that the captain always sat on the left and had assumed that, for a trial lesson, I would be sat on the right. In retrospect I should, of course, not have been surprised to be sat on the left as I was, after all, albeit for only an hour, the trainee pilot and there would be little point in learning to fly from the right seat when all the essential controls would be the wrong way round. I was also surprised that it was quite obvious from the start that I would have control of the aircraft throughout under the instructor's watchful eyes, despite the fact that I had no experience whatsoever in flying an aircraft.

The instructor handed me a checklist, detailing all the operations that were required prior to the start of the engine and we went through these slowly, one by one, to check all the aircraft systems and controls. He then gave me the key and told me to ìstart up the engineî. The engine fired without any problem but it was surprising to find that as soon as it did, the aircraft pitched nose down straining against the front wheel which the instructor explained was due to the propeller trying to pull us away against the main wheel brakes. The instructor made a quick radio call to the Airport Tower Controller, then we were ready for the off.

This is where the next surprise came. You do not steer an aircraft with the 'wheel' or as it should be called, the yoke, but you steer it with your feet using the rudder pedals. The rudder pedals are connected to a steerable nose wheel and toe brakes are mounted separately at the top of the pedals. It sounds difficult but it is actually relatively easy in a tricycle gear aircraft, i.e. one wheel at the front and two under the wings, once you get used to it, and having pushed the throttle lever gently forward to apply power we started to move away from the parking area up to the holding point at the start of the runway. Again, the instructor explained the meaning of the markings on the ground, the yellow line was to be followed as closely as possible and we were not to enter the runway without permission. Turning the aircraft into the wind to aid cooling of the engine we then performed what he called the run-up, which seemed a strange name at the time but basically what it entailed was bringing the engine up to a set RPM to check that all was well with the aircraft systems and engine including the oil system and the vacuum system which drives some of the instruments. You will need to refer to a more technical book for a full explanation of these. It is not the intention of this book to explain the inner workings of an aircraft.

Having completed all the pre-flight checks and being satisfied that all was well with the aircraft, the instructor called the Tower again and advised them that we were ready for departure following which we were given permission to enter the runway and take off. I still could not believe that I was actually going to perform this task but I was sure that the instructor knew what he was doing. Carefully taxiing out we lined up on the centreline, pointing straight down Newcastle International Airport's runway, which seemed to go on endlessly into the distance. Opening up the throttle fully we started off at what seemed a gentle pace but one that quickly became faster and faster, all the time steering with my feet to keep us in a straight line, until we reached a flying speed at which point the instructor told me to pull back gently but firmly on the yoke and we smoothly left the ground and started to climb away. I would like to think that I had actually carried out the entire take-off without assistance but I am sure that I felt the instructor manipulating the rudder pedals even though he had his hands well away from the yoke.

Learning to Fly in 21 Days

It was explained to me that airspeed is all important and to achieve a positive rate of climb a set speed should be aimed for and at what seemed like an acute angle into the sky we gradually gained height until we had reached 1,000 feet above the ground. I could not believe what I was actually doing but more importantly for me there were no signs of any problems and to say the least I was enjoying myself. Prior to taking off the instructor had asked me where I lived and it was obviously now the intention to take me over my house as he instructed me to gently turn the yoke right, which made the aircraft bank right and set us on course over the Tyne bridges and towards my house. The next forty minutes or so passed very quickly, during which time we did some gentle handling exercises, and tried to fly straight and level, then it was back to the airport.

The instructor reported our position to the Tower controller at Newcastle who gave us precise instructions and once in sight of the Airport we were cleared to land. I had assumed that the instructor would be landing the aircraft but again I was wrong. It was clearly his intention to give me full instructions on what to do and how to do it, and as we reduced height and came in on final approach I could see the runway approach lights which it was explained to me would indicate whether we were too high, or too low, on our approach and everything seemed to be going well. As we got closer to the ground however a call came from the Tower Controller which I did not understand. The instructor immediately took control of the aircraft and applying full power he banked us sharply away from the runway with the explanation that the police helicopter had requested an immediate and urgent departure from the airport and we had been instructed by the Tower to break off the approach and orbit in our present position.

A matter of minutes later we were on the ground, the instructor having kept control of the aircraft and my trial lesson was over. The first hurdle had been overcome, I had suffered no ill effects from being in a small aircraft and more positively I had really enjoyed it. I mentioned to the instructor what I was proposing to do, a three-week intensive course, and asked what he thought of my prospects to which he replied that I should have no problems, go and do it then go back and see him again.

And so on to the next hurdle, the CAA medical. This made me feel quite anxious. I had not seen a doctor for some time and whilst I felt fit and well there was always the nagging doubt that something could be wrong. Needless to say this anxiety was in immediate evidence when, to begin the examination, he took my blood pressure. The reading was abnormally high, not a very good start! The examiner asked me when I had last seen my own doctor and I explained that I had not actually seen him for some considerable time. I had not had a day off work for many years. The examiner decided that the high blood pressure was therefore probably due to the stress of the examination and suggested we try again at the end of the examination. Good decision. The rest of the examination went without a hitch, testing eyes for both sight and colour blindness, hearing, reflexes and all the other tests relevant to a full examination before returning to the question of my blood pressure. This time, having relaxed and calmed down, it was fine. Fifteen minutes later I had my CAA medical certificate. All I needed now was a Private Pilot's Licence to go with it.

From my earlier discussions with the proposed flight school I knew that there were two real parts to gaining the licence. There were the obvious practical aspects in addition to the technical aspects in terms of the written examinations. Bearing in mind the relatively short space of time within which I was proposing to achieve the practical side of the course, I wanted to make sure that I knew exactly what the requirements were for the written examinations. Perhaps more importantly I wanted to make some inroads into the actual studying to ensure that I would not be placed under undue stress whilst trying to learn to fly. I talked this through with the flight school when I telephoned to make the booking for my training and they gave me specific advice on the books and equipment that would be required. They also recommended that I should go out to Florida ready to sit at least three examinations, leaving three more to study for when not actually flying.

The major pilot equipment suppliers all offer packages to prospective pilots containing the books and equipment necessary and I would strongly recommend that you take advantage of these. I did not and I regretted it because I still ended up buying all the equipment separately despite having originally considered that I would not need it all. In terms of the books required for the written examinations, these may vary from time to time but I am sure that all relevant ones will be included in whatever package you decide on. In the main they are written by Trevor Thom in the series 'The Air Pilot's Manual'. One excellent additional book for use at the revision stage is the 'PPL Confuser' written by Glynn Stephens and compiled with the assistance of the Civil Aviation Authority which represents all of the questions used in the written examinations with model answers. One word of warning, do not attempt to use this book solely to gain the answers 'parrot fashion'. Flying is not a game and you need to have a good understanding of all subjects because one day your life may very well depend on it.

You will also need certain items of equipment such as a navigation plotter and ruler, flight computer and kneeboard, all of which should again be included in the packages offered by pilot suppliers. If they are not, then obviously you will need to purchase them separately and this is where a little caution comes in. The kneeboard is an invaluable piece of equipment and you should aim to purchase the best you can afford as it will serve you for years to come. I personally prefer a wallet style with hard frame in the middle and pockets that fold out either side and a strap that goes around your thigh to keep it in place. This gives a good writing surface which you will find is an invaluable advantage. The flight computer is a rather different story. It is actually similar to a slide rule and initially will seem complicated to use. My suggestion would be to buy the cheapest possible because whilst you do have to use it for your flight planning whilst undertaking the licence, as soon as you gain your PPL you will probably want to invest in an electronic one, similar to a calculator.

You will also need to have a good supply of pens and pencils together with different colour highlighters for marking your navigation charts. In the UK chinagraph pencils are also required which when used on the laminated style of chart can easily be wiped off again. The US however have paper charts, called Sectionals, and you are probably better off using the highlighters, or felt-tip pens, to mark your routes. Make sure that you also have a small notebook which will fit into the kneeboard pockets and which will be used to write down Air Traffic Control instructions and other notes during your training.

The final suggestion I would make to you concerns your preparation for the written examinations. I did a lot of studying in the two months prior to actually going to Florida and this paid off in the long run because all I had to do before sitting the actual examinations was revision. This was the case certainly for three of the subjects, Air Law, Human Factors and Pilot Performance, and Radio Telephony. In point of fact, with the changes in the training presently being introduced, it may be a requirement for you to hold a radio telephony licence before you can commence your training. You will need to seek guidance on this point from your local flight school. If you have no prior knowledge of radio telephony procedures then I would also recommend that you obtain an audio tape course, which you can play at home or in your car. This will greatly assist with many of the standard phrases used and prepare you for what to expect when you contact Air Traffic Controllers. If you have access to a computer there is a software product available, The 'PPL Exam Tutor', which I made use of during my studies. This gives a whole series of questions on all the examination subjects that you can take as a mock test and which give you details of right and wrong answers. Whatever books or other material that you purchase for you studies make sure they are up-to-date and designed for the new training syllabus.

So with preparation complete the final things to do are purchase a flying logbook ready to log all those training hours on the way to gaining your licence and book your flight. Make sure when you make your travel arrangements that you allow for the time differential and my strong suggestion to you would be to allow a full day to travel out to Florida and one extra day at the end giving yourself at the very least a full 21 days to complete the course.

Chapter Two

The First Five Days of Training

Having safely arrived in Florida the previous day, and been met at Orlando International Airport by the owners of my chosen flying school, the first day dawned on the start of my training. I was introduced to the instructor who would remain with me throughout the course, and quite apart from being a flying instructor he was also a qualified diving instructor and hang-gliding instructor. Little did I realise at this stage just how much I would rely on this instructor for support on a personal basis quite apart from the training aspect.

Having been introduced we sat down together and he explained to me exactly what the course entailed and how it would progress. Then it was out to the aircraft in which I would do the bulk of my training, a Cessna 150. It actually transpired that this aircraft, registration N66560, had been owned by my instructor although having decided he wished to sell it, the flying school had purchased it for student training so he was therefore in a good position to know the aircraft inside out.

The first task on the training was the external check of the aircraft, as clearly outlined in the aircraft manual, and this involved a logical walk around the aircraft checking all the relevant moving parts such as the ailerons and elevator, the landing gear and propeller, together with the general condition of the exterior. The engine was also checked in terms of oil level. As we walked around making the appropriate checks, the instructor explained how to do them and what to look for at each stage of the process.

Having completed the exterior checks it was into the aircraft, which after the trial flight in the four-seater Piper Cadet felt very cramped. The Cessna was a two-seater aircraft and as both the instructor and myself were quite well built it was certainly very cosy with literally no room between us. We were sat side by side, wedged in shoulder to shoulder. Having strapped ourselves in, the instructor handed me the check list to carry out the pre-start checks and, in much the same way as the trial lesson in Newcastle, it was made clear to me that I would be in control, unless some form of disaster struck. If this did happen, the instructor would assume control with the clear instruction "I have control" upon which I was to immediately release my hands and feet from the controls.

So there I was, 10 o'clock on the morning of a beautiful, bright and sunny day, out in Florida, with twenty-one days of flight training in front of me and hopefully at the end to return home with a Private Pilotís Licence. At that stage I did not realise the pain, anxiety and stress that would ensue during that period. But anyway, back to the first morning. Whilst the flying school has since moved to a new training facility at Winter Haven airfield, at the time I did my training it was based at Bartow about six miles to the south. Fig. 1. This was Class D controlled airspace complete with tower. I realised that in many ways learning to fly at a tower-controlled airfield rather than at one of the numerous uncontrolled airfields in Florida would stand me in good stead

View from the control tower of the flight school used for training - the school has since moved to a larger modern building at Winter Haven

for when I returned to the UK where I would have to cope with flying from Newcastle International Airport.

The instructor explained to me that there were two radio frequencies at Bartow, one for 'Ground' which as the name suggests controlled all movement on the ground at the airfield and the other for ëTowerí who would give take-off and landing clearances. The anomaly was that both frequencies were operated by the same controller who merely had two different radio sets, one on each side of him. Woe betides you however if you contacted him on the wrong frequency! So, I contacted 'Ground' and asked for permission to taxi to the active runway for departure. What came back over the radio was totally incomprehensible, at least to me. I had been warned that this controller would talk extremely fast and to be ready to write down what he said. The problem was that he spoke so fast, in the absence of good shorthand, I had no chance of writing any of it down! The instructor told me to key the mike and acknowledge the instructions received but I was totally dumbstruck. I had absolutely no idea what the controller had just said to me. As it transpired he had given me basic instructions to taxi the aircraft to a runway together with information on the prevailing winds and altimeter setting. This problem with understanding the controller's instructions was to haunt me for days to come. With the instructor having read back the instruction to the controller we duly taxied to the holding point, in the same manner as at Newcastle, to perform the run-up engine checks.

This is, however, perhaps an opportune moment to mention the difference between the way the UK and US express their altimeter settings. The UK defines pressure in millibars and the US in inches of mercury. The direct comparisons are that standard pressure in the UK is expressed as 1013mb and in the US this equates to 29.92in. This is easy to get used to and in any event UK and US altimeters are calibrated using the respective measurements.

With these checks completed and the frequency on the radio changed to 'Tower' it was time to contact the controller for permission to depart. All of these actions would be repeated numerous times over the course of the next three weeks and whilst initially, as I have said, I am sure the controller tried to talk as fast as possible to confuse the students, eventually his instructions became more meaningful and easier to interpret only however, once I had a basic understanding of what to actually expect him to say to me when I asked him for something. This was, I have to admit, not my strong point over the first few days but more on that later.

As I have said previously, the emphasis in my training right from day one was on having control. So as I carefully taxied us out on the runway, lined up on the centreline, and opened the throttle, the aircraft immediately started to roll forward. Careful use of the rudder pedals was an absolute must to keep us in a straight line. Once we had reached sufficient speed the instructor told me to pull back gently on the yoke and as I did we climbed away from the ground.

This first lesson concentrated on the effect of all the flying controls and the basic aspects of keeping the aircraft flying straight and level on headings defined by the instructor. At this stage, as indeed was the case for probably the next ten days or so, I could really have been flying anywhere as my concentration was entirely focused on flying the aircraft. I had no real idea of where I was in relation to the airfield and this is definitely something that I should have been more aware of as it would have certainly eased the pain considerably when later in the course it came to actual navigation. Take my word for it, it will be invaluable!

I know that this is something that is difficult to be aware of, but unlike flying from your local airfield in the UK where you probably know many of the landmarks, flying in Florida, or indeed any strange place, is made more difficult when you have no local knowledge. This is something that you should make a real effort to gain as soon as you can.

Having spent nearly an hour and a half in the air, getting used to the basic effects of the flying controls it was time to return to Bartow for a de-brief and ground school. Contact was made with the Tower for permission to enter the airspace and the controller issued instructions that again were so fast that I had no idea what he was talking about.

As it transpired he had issued me with instructions on entering his airspace and given a position from where he wished me to report from prior to landing. Having duly reported in and been given permission to land, the instructor advised that he had control but that I was to follow his actions through on the controls for the first landing of my training to see exactly how it was done.

He explained that under normal circumstances the ideal landing is made as close as possible to the stall speed of the aircraft, the speed at which it loses the ability to fly. He then proceeded to talk me through the process making a wonderfully soft landing with a quiet squeak of the tyres on touchdown.

After landing the aircraft the controller then issued what seemed at the time to be a rather strange instruction, 'taxi to the ramp and monitor ground'. What was he talking about? The first part was obvious but surely he did not think that I would taxi the aircraft without looking where I was going? Then of course the penny dropped. It was this anomaly again of one man and two radios on the ground I had to monitor the Ground frequency!

Having parked the aircraft and shut down the engine it was back into the flight school for a de-brief. I was feeling very good after this first flight which, as far as I was concerned, had gone very well. The instructor seemed pleased enough although he did pass the opinion that I was perhaps concentrating too much on the flight instruments in controlling the aircraft and that I would have to learn to fly more by feel and sound and generally relax.

When I look back now that was extremely sound advice and the fact that I did not take it on board at the time probably gave rise to some of the problems I encountered over the next week or so. It certainly would have helped me in the next flight later on that day.

Taking off again in mid-afternoon it was immediately obvious that this was going to be a totally different experience to the morning flight. Something that I had not considered at any of my stages of preparation for undertaking the course was that at that time of year in Florida, in early June, the afternoons are very hot and sticky with the temperature rising substantially throughout the day. This causes thermals and turbulence in the air.

This had an immediate impact on my flying resulting in my having great difficulty in keeping control of the aircraft, and I appeared to be constantly fighting with the controls. The instructor advised me again that I should try and relax. He assured me that the only hold I should have on the yoke was between finger and thumb of the left hand and I should not handle the yoke as though I was driving a car. Despite what I now know was good advice, that a light touch is all that is needed, I continued to struggle. The aircraft seemed to have a mind of its own and was bouncing around all over the place in the air, not only from side to side but also vertically in the turbulent thermals.

As time went on I began to lose confidence entirely, feeling totally incapable of controlling the aircraft, even after climbing up to 6,000 feet into cooler air to try and remove the obvious problems. It was one depressed student who returned to Bartow on that first day having received a total of three hours and ten minutes flying instruction.

That night I did not sleep very well. The realisation of the enormous task that I had set out to achieve finally registered and I was left with great nagging doubts about my ability to actually complete the course.

Up early on day two and into the flight school for a briefing with the instructor on the next lesson and an overview of yesterday's events. The instructor assured me that the problems I had encountered were common to most students and that it would take time to get used to the feel of flying and to stop trying to fight with the controls.

Turning final approach for runway 04 at Winter Haven airfield

Out to the aircraft and after the usual pre-flight exterior checks it was time to contact 'Ground' for permission to taxi the aircraft out to the runway. Again, the standard staccato response came back from the controller which left me totally unable to make out anything meaningful from what I had just heard and I had to rely on my instructor for a translation before keying the mike and reading back the clearance.

After performing all the pre-flight checks and run-up and a further one sided conversation with the 'Tower' controller we were back up in the early morning still air, a great difference from yesterday afternoon. Once again the lesson concentrated on the core basic aspects of flying, straight and level, ascents and descents and medium level turns.

A word of advice here. Volume One of the Air Pilot's manual, 'Flying Training', describes all the practical exercises in some detail and it is worth studying this well in advance of your lessons in order that you can be prepared mentally for what is actually entailed.

We then headed for Winter Haven airfield, which is not controlled by a Tower, to do some practice take-offs and landings. In the United States there are many airfields which are uncontrolled and which use what is called a Unicom frequency to transmit 'blind' traffic information for the benefit of other pilots. The only problem with this system is that many airfields use the same frequencies and this can be disconcerting until you get used to it. Take-offs were adequate as far as I was concerned but this was to be the first real attempt at landing an aircraft myself and it showed.

My performance can only be described as abysmal. I could not gauge just how far above the runway we were before attempting to slow the aircraft down by pulling back on the yoke and raising the nose prior to touchdown: in flying terms the round-out or flare. The instructor demonstrated how it should be done and what to look for when landing but it just would not come together and almost inevitably he would end up taking control at the last minute in order to avoid disaster.

His advice was to avoid looking at the near runway but look right down it, which I know is the advice given in all the text books, but I was fixated on the near end of the runway which resulted in a hard or bounced landing every time. After a number of attempts the instructor decided enough was enough for the time being so it was back to Bartow where inevitably the instructor took control at the last minute to avert another disaster. At least confidence had been restored in my general flying skills but obviously my landings were going to require a lot of work.

After lunch I had an appointment to see the local Federal Aviation Administration Medical Examiner. Despite the fact that I already held a CAA medical certificate it is necessary as a student pilot to undergo an FAA medical before being allowed to fly solo in US airspace and indeed, this certificate also acts as your student pilot licence. This examination did not fill me with the same level of dread and trepidation that the equivalent CAA examination had previously done and needless to say this second medical examination went without a hitch.

In late afternoon once back at Bartow, it was again time to brave those thermals and off we went straight to Winter Haven to try and improve my landings without the worry of having to contend with Tower controlled airspace. At this point it should be obvious that the radio work had given me a great deal of problems.

You will remember earlier that the controller at Bartow gave instructions so fast over the radio that they were difficult to comprehend and more often than not, whilst I had clearly heard what he had said, it went straight into my head and out again. I was therefore unable to read back to him any of the instructions and information that he had just told me.

Effectively I found myself totally dumbstruck. It was starting to improve on the ground where at least I could write down what I had heard as I was getting used to receiving virtually the same instructions each time, but in the air, trying to maintain control of the aircraft, I seemed to need an extra pair of hands. I could not seem to fly, listen and write at the same time.

Part of the problem I later discovered was the lack of a kneeboard. This is why I gave the advice in the first chapter that this really is an essential piece of equipment. Only after I had purchased my own kneeboard locally did the problem of being able to write something down at the same time as fly the aircraft diminish. That still however left the problem of actually understanding what it was he was telling me in the first place!

Having managed to find Winter Haven, which is only six miles from Bartow and virtually due north, it was back into those practice landings again. They were slowly starting to improve but they were not yet consistent. They seemed to be more through luck than judgement for I had still not got into the idea of looking down the runway and finding a spot on the windshield that would indicate when we were about to touchdown.

This really was a problem of perspective because whilst on the ground although I obviously knew what the view out of the window should look like I was unable to visualise that same perspective when approaching to land. Everything then seemed to happen so fast which resulted in my nearly always coming in and trying to land too high above the runway leaving the aircraft to effectively drop what seemed like the last few feet onto the ground. With the benefit of hindsight this is another important lesson worth learning. If I had paid greater attention to this perspective whilst on the ground it would probably have improved my landings in a shorter space of time.

After a number of practice attempts it seemed that they were not improving at all; I could not gauge the final few feet to the runway and inevitably I appeared to drop the aircraft down in a hard or bounced landing. It is perhaps a good thing that the undercarriage of a Cessna is said to be so forgiving! Despite the lack of finesse in evidence, the one good thing was that the instructor must have thought they were starting to improve as he was no longer taking control at the last minute in order to avoid a disaster. Looking back now I dread to think what the landings where he did take control would have been like had he not done so.

So day two ended with a further three hours' instruction giving me a total of six hours and ten minutes in my logbook.

Day three did not start well. We had flown to Winter Haven to again work on take-offs and landings and it was painfully obvious that they were not improving at all. Apart from which, with the limited time available between each take-off and landing my use of the radio to make the required position calls within the circuit was appalling. I was totally confused at the whereabouts of our position within each stage of the circuit between take-off and landing and this was having a disastrous effect on my flying. My brain seemed unable to cope with doing so many different things in such a short space of time, each circuit probably only taking in the region of ten minutes from initial take-off to landing again.

Sensing my extreme frustration, and obviously witnessing my total incompetence, the instructor finally agreed that the only way out of this would be for him, for the time being, to make the radio calls and allow me to concentrate on actually flying the aircraft. Whilst this did relieve the workload somewhat it really only had a marginal effect on my landings. I was still experiencing difficulty in judging the height of the aircraft above the ground, a consequence of which was that the landing always seemed to give me a panic attack which understandably resulted in either a hard or a bounced landing each time. It seemed to me at the time that the runway appeared to move at the very last minute from where I expected it to be!

Flying the actual circuit after initial take-off was beginning to show signs of improvement and with the instructor making the radio position calls these were starting to register in my mind. I could fly the aircraft relatively successfully until lined up on final approach when the aircraft seemed to develop a mind of its own and would drift from side to side as we got closer to the ground. The closer we got to touchdown the more I seemed to tense up and instead of holding the aircraft off the ground until it was ready to give up flying on its own accord, I seemed to manage to drop it onto the runway before it was ready.

Part of the problem for me seemed to be the changing perspective and attitude of the aircraft when the flaps were applied ready for landing. The normal routine was to apply the first stage at the end of the downwind leg and trim the aircraft for a constant speed and descent rate. When the next stages of flap were applied on final approach these always seemed to throw the nose down towards the ground giving the impression of landing nose first.

In actual fact this was a totally mistaken perception because in the final stages of landing, with the round-out and flare, these would bring the aircraft into a nose-high attitude and allow the main wheels only to touch the ground first. The problem was I could not judge the correct height before flaring, possibly because of the fear of landing or even crashing into the ground nose first.

The afternoon's lesson did nothing to improve my confidence. We had flown to the airfield at Lake Wales, another uncontrolled airport 11 miles to the south-east of Bartow, and that afternoon the wind was gusting to fifteen knots which was obviously not going to help my landings. If I could not manage a decent landing in relatively calm winds how was I going to cope with this strength of wind? The simple answer was that I wasn't. Crosswinds were for me a new phenomenon and from the outset I was not comfortable.

Whilst flying the circuit this time, instead of flying relatively straight, it was obviously necessary to adjust for the wind in order to maintain a constant distance from the airfield. This was not a pleasant experience. It involved crabbing the aircraft sideways through the air and the perspective on landing was totally different. Instead of setting up on final approach and looking straight ahead and down the runway, this time the runway appeared to be off to one side the technique being to straighten the aircraft up just before touchdown by applying corrective rudder.

All very well in theory but as I could not gauge the height above the runway in the first place this brought a new potential dimension into the things that could go wrong. And of course they did. Inevitably as before I flared too high above the runway, and of course expecting to imminently touch down, also applied the corrective rudder too early which meant that I drifted with the prevailing wind across the runway. Good job that those runways were so wide!

After an hour of struggling to control the aircraft it was back to Bartow for what can only be described as my worst landing up to that point. I managed to virtually stall the aircraft just above the runway which meant that we dropped onto the runway like a helicopter with engine failure rather than landing like a light aircraft.

That afternoon I felt totally and utterly despondent. Despite my intention to sit several of the written examinations during the early stages of the course, I had not done so. With regard to my flying, or more importantly my landings, there was no sign whatsoever of any improvement, or indeed that I was actually learning from my mistakes. I was effectively overloaded with information and procedures and I was experiencing major difficulty in coping.

So at the end of day three, with another two hours and fifty minutes flying time in my logbook, making a grand total of nine hours instruction, there appeared to be very little improvement in my overall standard, certainly where landing the aircraft was involved.

The next day, feeling the same as I had the previous day I had already decided that day four should be spent on concentrating on the theory side of the licence rather than on the actual flying. My instructor agreed that perhaps the morning lesson could be spent practising basic exercises in the air rather than continuous take-off and landing practice, and then in the afternoon, perhaps I could concentrate on sitting some of the written examinations.

It transpired that although this was all very well in theory, the weather conspired against me as the wind strength increased steadily over the morning leaving me, once again, fighting to maintain control of the aircraft in the air. The intention had been to work on my general airmanship, including flying straight and level at a defined altitude together with climbing and descending turns from one altitude to another. With the wind as it was, I was having great difficulty in even staying straight in level flight let alone climbing and descending accurately to a new altitude! After two hours I was both physically and mentally exhausted.

My instructor did however give me a great deal of encouragement in suggesting that I should also look at the Federal Aviation Administration pre-flight solo written examination covering the basic requirements of FAA law and a prerequisite for a student before a solo flight in US airspace. Not a difficult exam, it can be taken with the benefit of the FAA Regulations and Aeronautical Information Manual (FAR-AIM) and after an hour or so of study I duly passed it.

Still early afternoon and therefore plenty of time to make inroads into the other written examinations. After an intensive period of revision I took both Air Law and Human Performance and passed without any problems. At least the day ended on a high note. Even if I was still having trouble with the practical aspects of flying at least my technical knowledge was good. Total flying time on day four was two hours and five minutes giving a total in my logbook now of eleven hours and five minutes instruction.

The next morning, once again, did not start well. We had flown to Lake Wales to try and sort out my landing problems but we were hampered somewhat by the activities of the sky-diving club also based at the field. For obvious safety reasons we stayed well away from the airfield and instead we worked on further manoeuvres in the air. As well as general handling of the aircraft, flying straight and level, ascents and descents with and without power and medium turns, we also looked at what for me were more complex manoeuvres.

These included flying around a fixed point on the ground at a constant distance and height to take account of the wind direction, together with flying constant S-bends in the air using a straight road as a reference. These manoeuvres went extremely well and it finally seemed as if I was actually starting to improve my handling of the aircraft, at least when the wind was calm. It was still those landings that were giving me great cause for concern because unless they started to improve there was a real risk as far as I could envisage, of never being capable of flying solo. This was understandably beginning to result in my having serious emotional stress.

With the sky-diving activity apparently finished at Lake Wales we headed back over to the airfield to again practise my landings. As it transpired this was probably the worst thing that we could have done after the earlier success of the flight manoeuvres. The actual circuit, at least up to the final approach, was no longer giving me cause for concern. It seemed however that in the final stages of landing I could not get rid of the tension that I felt which was obviously clouding my mental judgement of perspective. I was now landing badly for a number of different reasons. I either hit the runway hard, bounced down the runway in a little series of mini landings or I was either too fast or too slow in the final stages of the approach.

Following three atrocious landings and the joint frustration at my performance being vented verbally by both my instructor and myself, my emotional state deteriorated to such an extent I told the instructor that I wanted to call it a day. After a totally silent return to Bartow the instructor could obviously sense my depression was extreme. After parking and tying down the aircraft, rather than return to the flight school we went into the airport offices to get a coffee and sit down and talk this problem through.

He asked me quite pointedly if I was considering giving up the course and said that if I was he thought I would be a total fool. He told me that I should expect at least one day a week when everything would totally fall apart simply because of the amount of instruction that was necessary if the course was to be completed in full in the three weeks. He also attempted to reassure me that whilst my landings were not that good, my general flying was improving in terms of the required air manoeuvres.

He then suggested that I should spend the rest of the day reviewing the art of landing an aircraft from the text books and at the same time try and view the video the school had that established exactly what the logical order of events of landing an aircraft were. This would also hopefully help me establish the perspective view of the runway that would tell me that I was on a good approach. He also advised me that I must relax, that flying is not difficult to learn and that by being so tense in the final stages of landing I was in effect defeating myself. I expected them to go wrong and they did. It was the classic self-fulfilling prophecy.

All of this understandably gave me a great deal to think about. I had no intention of admitting defeat but I have to confess that at that time I was thoroughly depressed with my perceived lack of improvement. I had however come to Florida with the sole intention of learning to fly and that was exactly what I was going to do. I took his advice and located the 'Better Landings' video in the flight school and settled down to watch this in conjunction with Trevor Thom's 'Air Pilot's Manual, Volume One'. Whether these would make any difference to my landings would only be apparent the next day.

Arriving back at the house where I was staying with other students from the school my despondency must have been self-evident. One of the students, who already held the basic pilot licence and was in Florida to undertake the instrument flying course, offered a great deal of encouragement and advice. He also effectively took my mind off the situation by giving me some practical instruction on the use of the flight computer. Up to this stage I had not needed to use it, this would come when planning the navigation exercises later in the course, although I have to admit that trying to do any calculations on it had left me in some initial difficulty. Once he had shown me in practical terms how it should be used, rather than trying to work it out from the complicated instruction manual, it became a lot easier to understand. I would strongly suggest to you that you try and find someone who knows how to use one of these and get him or her to show you practically how it works rather than try and find out from the manual on its own.

So at the end of the fifth day, which can only be described as the worst day so far, with a further one hour and thirty minutes flying time I now had a total of twelve hours and thirty-five minutes instruction.

Chapter Three

Day Six to Day Ten of the Training

Following the events of yesterday I was not looking forward to day six as this could well turn out to be a defining moment in my training. As it transpired it was quite an overcast day but the wind was relatively calm and my instructor was convinced that it would be a good day in my training and it was in this buoyant mood, at least on his part, that we set off up to the airfield at Winter Haven.

My instructor explained that he had decided we would do three practice circuits. I would fly the aircraft whilst he would handle the radio calls, but on final approach I was to let him have control at which stage he would not actually land but would fly the aircraft down the length of the runway a matter of inches off the ground. Whilst he was doing that I was to concentrate solely on the perspective view both in front and to the side and consciously in my mind mark a spot on the windshield as a reference point whilst following through his actions on the controls. With my hands and feet resting lightly on the yoke and rudder pedals respectively the first approach was made as if we were going to land but right at the last minute, the instructor applied power and we flew at what seemed like extremely low level down half the length of the runway before climbing away again. This had indeed given me the chance to gain a true perspective in the final moments before touchdown and using the same reference point on the windshield for the second and third approaches confirmed that I now had a constant indicator that I could use.

After these three demonstrations the instructor handed control of the aircraft back to me and it was time now to see whether I had actually learnt anything. Much to my surprise it transpired that I had. I was now concentrating on visualising the perspective demonstrated previously and whilst the first landing was not exactly perfect it was certainly a vast improvement on my previous efforts.

The second improved on the first and by the time I got to landing number five they were actually starting to become consistent. Not entirely 'greasers', the term given to absolutely perfect landings, but on a scale of one to five they may have warranted a three which was a considerable improvement on the previous score of zero!

We spent the next two hours just practising take-offs and landings during which time it became obvious, at least to me, that I had actually learnt something. My landings were slowly improving and we were no longer ballooning above the ground or bouncing down the runway. For good measure my instructor actually demonstrated a practice go-around, the action taken when breaking off an approach for some reason.

This did not afford me with any real problems as of course in a go-around I did not have to actually land the aircraft! The only thing to be wary of is the potential sharp attitude change when full power is applied because the nose of the aircraft immediately wants to balloon skyward and it is actually necessary to forcibly hold the yoke forward to avoid a potential stall situation.

After the events of the previous day my spirit had returned as well as my confidence and it is only a shame that we had not considered the low-pass approach sooner. My obvious advice to you, if you experience the same sort of problems, is ask your instructor to at least try the same method. It may well work for you as indeed it did for me.

Following the vast improvement seen in my landings, the return to Bartow after two hours and twenty minutes instruction saw me in high spirits. The only damper was that the weather had started to close in. Thunderstorms were forecast along with rain for the next twenty-four to thirty-six hours so there was to be no more flying that day which to me was an obvious shame bearing in mind the substantial improvement that had been achieved.

The only downside at this stage of my training was that I still had to cope with making the radio calls whilst flying the aircraft before my instructor would consider me capable of flying solo. Like my landings these seemed to have come on in leaps and bounds, at least in the circuit, and I could now make the correct calls in the appropriate places. I was however still having problems in dealing with the controller at Bartow. I had started to recognise the various instructions and reporting points that he would give before allowing me to enter his airspace but for some reason, whilst I could hear what he said, and by this stage could write it down on my kneeboard, invariably it seemed that I became totally tongue-tied when it came to reading back the instructions.

My instructor suggested that this was really a question of being prepared in advance. Depending on the wind direction I should be able to anticipate which runway would be in use, and by listening to other pilots communicating with the controller I should be able to pick up the other information that he would pass in his call to me. Logical thinking but I was having enough problems in listening to and interpreting the controller's transmissions to me without trying to decipher those that he was making to other pilots!

Following the obvious high of the morning, I started revising for a further two examinations in the afternoon, Aircraft Technical and Radio Telephony, the latter of which seemed entirely appropriate bearing in mind the problems I was having. These were duly passed meaning that I now had only two more to go, Navigation and Meteorology, and this, certainly from a mental point of view set me back on track to where I had originally planned to be at this point. Overall it was a good sixth day which certainly made up for day five which is best forgotten. Total instruction was now fourteen hours and fifty-five minutes.

As it transpired the weather forecast was quite accurate and day seven started with an overcast sky and a cloud base at 400 feet and so it was obvious there would be no flying in the immediate future. My instructor decided that this would make a good day to concentrate on groundschool so we looked at some basic map reading, course planning and distance, and time and fuel calculations together with details of how to calculate weight and balance. The time also gave me an opportunity to do some more studying for the meteorology examination, the only time I had spent so far on this particular subject was on the eight-hour flight from Gatwick to Orlando meaning that I had, of course, missed out on the in-flight entertainment!

Bearing in mind the weather, my instructor considered that it might be a good time to go and talk to the Tower controller about the general radio calls and as it transpired that was a really good idea. The controller was very pleased to show me around, and despite his staccato-like radio manner, in person he was totally different. He was more than happy to go through with me the system that he used to control aircraft within his airspace, and more importantly for me, the entry procedures that he used for aircraft joining the circuit.

This was of enormous benefit to me as it now meant that I could at least have some idea of what the controller would say to me in the air prior to him actually issuing the instruction. Having met him it also meant that our subsequent radio communications would have a more personal feel rather than just anonymous exchanges over the radio. This last aspect was to prove of great value. He obviously appreciated our discussion regarding my general problems with handling radio communications and agreed that provided I always started my initial radio call with "good morning" or "good afternoon" he would make a conscious effort to slow down his rate of speech!

The weather did not improve at all in the afternoon and in the event I was unable to do any flying at all that day, total instruction would remain at fourteen hours and fifty five minutes although this is still an average over the first week of over two hours each day, and well in excess of what I could have expected to achieve in the UK. My confidence had also been restored in terms of my practical flying skills and this, combined with getting four of the written examinations out of the way, meant that I considered I was back on track to achieve the licence within the remaining two weeks.

The weather at the start of day eight was still not very good with early morning haze and a low cloud base, so it was into more groundschool on navigation and the use of the flight computer. Having previously received some informal instruction from a fellow student it was relatively simple to make the necessary calculations for flight planning. These included calculations of the variations between indicated air speed and actual ground speed together with the divergence between the track over the ground and the actual true heading to allow for the wind direction and speed.

By late morning the weather had started to clear and so it was up into the air again to try and consolidate on the experience gained a couple of days ago. True to his word, upon using "good morning" on first contact with the Tower controller, the instructions that came back were spoken considerably slower

The control tower at Bartow - home of the friendly controller!

giving me the chance to actually retain in my mind what was being said. The instructor found this change in the controller's style highly amusing, I just hoped that the controller would retain this sympathy for me for the duration of my training!

The actual break from flying on the previous day had given me a chance to relax and relieved some of the pressure of flying each day. This was certainly in evidence in my general flying but more importantly in the noticeable improvement in my landings. I no longer had the panic attacks during the last stages of the approach and confidence in my eventual success had now been restored.

The concentration for this lesson was to bring me up to the required standard for my first solo and together with simulated go-arounds, the procedure to abort an attempted landing in the final stages of approach, we also practised power-off glide approaches and simulated engine failures after take-off in order for my instructor to be sure that I could safely handle the aircraft, at least for one circuit, on my own.

Whilst my general landings had improved considerably these were only when the wind was virtually straight down the runway or where there was virtually no wind at all. I was still having problems with crosswind landings. It always seemed peculiar to be on final approach to land with the aircraft pointed away to one side, crabbing into the wind, and I was having trouble gauging exactly when to apply rudder and straighten the aircraft up seconds before touchdown. I knew the correct techniques, I had watched them on the video countless times already where the pilot in the video made it look so easy, but once again I was having difficulty in translating theory into practice.

My instructor at this stage was also insisting that my landings became more accurate in terms of being directly on the centre line of the runway, and within a defined distance from the threshold. Up to this time in my training we had been using the airfields at Lake Wales and Winter Haven as well as the home base of Bartow for all the landing practice where the runways were all well in excess of 4,000 feet long, considerably more than actually required to safely land the little Cessna 150. Sooner or later I would have to get used to landing on runways that could be considerably shorter and this is where accuracy would be vital.

Unfortunately by the afternoon the weather started to close in again with further thunderstorms building. Bearing in mind the only remaining prerequisite before I could even be considered to be allowed to fly solo was recognising and recovering from stalls and incipient spins, together with handling abnormally slow flying, this would now have to be left until the next day.

Flying instruction for day eight amounted to one hour and twenty-five minutes. Somewhat less than I was hoping for having missed the previous day but this still brought my total instruction time up to sixteen hours and twenty minutes.

Day nine dawned bright and sunny with an early start in the air. My instructor and I flew down to Lake Wales to build on the emergency procedures we had looked at the previous day and although once again we were interrupted by sky-divers over the airfield leading to a brief break in my instruction, the lesson itself did go very well. The landings now appear to be consistent, not brilliant, but passable, and even the cross-wind landings were starting to improve. I was also getting more used to actually judging the spot on which the aircraft would land and overall I was feeling very confident. My use of the radio was also steadily improving and making the required calls, at least in the circuit, was beginning to become second nature to me.

All that was now left before potentially my first solo flight was slow flying, and stalls and incipient spins. For obvious reasons these have to be practised at a safe height so it was up to 5,000 feet to carry out this lesson. Slow flying requires the aircraft to be flown at the slowest possible speed, just above the stall when the wings produce insufficient lift to allow the aircraft to fly. This was to cause no real problems for me but when it came to the actual stall itself this was something totally different because I did not have the faintest idea what would actually happen.

My instructor gave me specific instructions on how to recover from a stall, but looking back now it would have been far better if he had demonstrated one first. At least it would have prepared me somewhat for the shock to come. Before I describe to you what actually happened, let me recommend that you get your instructor to demonstrate one first.

My instructor told me to close the throttle removing all power and to maintain height through pulling back on the yoke to increase the angle of attack of the wings. It soon seemed as though we were practically facing vertically up into the sky. Then it started. With the stall-warning horn blaring, the aircraft seemed to shake all over and before I knew it we had tipped violently sideways in the sky and were plummeting towards the earth. For the first time in my training I was really genuinely frightened because with hindsight I was totally unprepared for the sudden reaction of the aircraft.

As we plunged towards the ground the instructor obviously took control so we were soon flying straight and level again whilst he explained exactly what had happened. He told me that at the moment of the stall the wings had not been level and as I sensed this, rather than using the rudder to keep the aircraft balanced, I had actually applied aileron. This had precipitated an incipient spin. He had then taken the corrective action of applying full opposite rudder to stop the aircraft spinning.

Regardless of why and how it had occurred the exercise had shaken me badly. I had no immediate wish to try it again although of course, like all of the training, it was something that

I would eventually have to master if I was to gain my private pilot's licence. My instructor decided to continue this particular lesson with some instrument flying using what is popularly known as the 'hood' which fits onto your head and obscures all view outside of the aircraft. The only thing that remains visible is the instrument panel in front of you.

Bearing in mind the fact that I had previously been fixated on the instruments rather than looking outside of the aircraft and gaining a visual perspective to my flying, this was no real problem even though it did involve intense concentration which actually took my mind off the early part of the lesson.

After half an hour or so we had climbed back to 5,000 feet and it was time to try those now dreaded stalls again. This time my instructor demonstrated one first explaining the importance of keeping the wings level and the aircraft balanced at such a slow airspeed. After the same blaring stall-warning noise and the shaking of the airframe the aircraft stalled but this time it was a much gentler affair. The nose broke towards the ground but at least with the wings still level and no sign of a spin. So it was back to me to try again.

With my feet anxiously worked the rudder pedals to keep the wings straight and level, and now being fully prepared for what would happen, it was a better experience. It wasn't exactly what I would call enjoyable, but it was something that at least I felt I could cope with. My instructor did explain to me however that that was not the end of it. More practice would be required under different situations such as a full-power stall, a power-off stall, and a stall with and without flaps. All of these would of course be undertaken early the next day in preparation for my first solo.

As I came to the end of day nine, even with the initial shock of my first experience of a stall it had been a relatively good day with three hours and fifteen minutes instruction now bringing the total up to nineteen hours and thirty-five minutes It was therefore fingers crossed for an even better day tomorrow!

So we come to day ten, Friday the thirteenth! The day started clear and bright but the forecast for later on in the day was not so good with the potential for thunderstorms again. It remained to be seen whether I could satisfy my instructor sufficiently for him to send me off on my first solo. After a number of take-offs and landings we headed off south from Bartow, down over the open countryside to practice the emergency procedures for an engine failure in flight and forced landings together with slow flight, stalls and incipient spins.

We spent some time going over the various stall configurations and whilst I was initially filled with dread, with one exception where the wing dropped again and we started a spin, they all went well and my instructor seemed to be pleased with my progress. Perhaps of more importance to me was the fact that I now felt happy with my performance and had the confidence that I could actually handle the aircraft.

The only problem was the weather. It had slowly been getting darker and darker throughout the morning with ominous black clouds looming. It was obvious that a storm would soon break so it was back to Bartow to sit it out on the ground.

With the bad weather being forecast for the rest of the day, my instructor decided that as we had already completed nearly two hours flying that morning, we would call it a day and aim for my first solo early the next day. Probably a good idea bearing in mind the date! As it transpired the owner of the flight school had other ideas which were not to become evident until somewhat later that day.

Following my instructor's departure I settled down for the afternoon to study for the remaining two written examinations, Meteorology and Navigation, which were probably quite appropriate when you bear in mind the torrential rain that was falling outside. However at about 4.30 p.m. the rain stopped and the sky cleared at which point the owner of the school, who was also the examiner, interrupted my studies by telling me that he wanted to see for himself how I was doing. Little did I realise what the next hour would bring!

We set out from Bartow and flew up to Winter Haven and despite my extreme nervousness of flying with the man who would eventually decide, as my examiner, whether I would gain my licence, he did put me at my ease and everything actually went quite well with my landings. We did three 'touch-and-go' landings and a practice go-around and then he told me to do a full stop landing, a landing where you actually bring the aircraft to a full stop on the runway, taxi off and back up to the hold point and then take off again.

We did two of these and on the third just as we were at the hold and I was completing all the final checks to enter the runway and take off again, he reached down, pulled his headset jacks out from the radio box, opened the door and as he got out of the aircraft turned and said to me "Right, time to go it alone".

To say I was stunned would be an understatement but incredibly this seemed to be it. The time had actually come for me to make my first solo flight. I must have been on some sort of autopilot for I only vaguely remember finishing the final checks and taxiing out to line up on the runway before opening up the throttle fully.

With the owner's departure from the aircraft a significant amount of weight was now out of the aircraft and so it accelerated rapidly down the runway and fairly leapt into the air. In what appeared to be a far quicker time than I was used to I had climbed up to circuit height, 1000 feet above the ground. Once there it was time to level off and concentrate on getting back down to the ground again, on my own and in one piece.

Completing all the pre-landing checks I reduced power at the appropriate stage in the circuit which had been drummed into me so many times over the past ten days, abeam the runway numbers on the downwind leg, and throttling back the engine slowed the aircraft down so that the initial stage of flaps could be lowered. As I turned the aircraft onto the final stages of the approach it looked good, not too high and not too low, and the airspeed pegged at the correct approach speed for landing.

I could see the school's owner standing by the side of the runway about half way down and just hoped that this would be a good landing. As it turned out it was, and in fact it was probably the best I had achieved so far. Stopping the aircraft off the runway and picking up the owner I was absolutely delighted that I had now achieved what is the first goal for all pilots, the first solo. I flew back to Bartow in a state of shock. Needless to say there was cause for much celebration that night.

I had now completed a further three hours dual flying, but in addition I now had an initial fifteen minutes solo time. This brought the total time in my log book to twenty-two hours and fifty minutes.

Administration building at Winter Haven airfield.

Chapter Four

Day Eleven to Day Fifteen of the Training

My confidence had understandably improved following yesterday's first solo flight and so it was up into the air early with my instructor for a check-ride that went extremely well. After just one circuit he stepped out of the aircraft to enable me to start making inroads into the required five hours of purely flying solo circuits. This was necessary before I could proceed to the next stage of my flying instruction, the cross-country work.

After the stress of the first ten days of the course which had lead up to my first solo, I knew the next few days would seem relatively peaceful whilst I gained the necessary solo hours and built on the experience gained so far. There is not really much I can comment on about this first real session of solo flying save for the fact that it was very hot and sticky, probably the hottest day experienced so far, despite being well before ten o'clock in the morning, and inevitably the first round of solo work did not last very long.

I realised that I needed to drink plenty of fluid for I was conscious of the intense perspiration flooding from my brow, partly due to the heat but more possibly due to the intense concentration required for the circuit work which unlike previously was now being carried out in the controlled airspace of Bartow. At least my friendly controller in the Tower was still showing a great deal of patience with my radio work! After a short break, and a further check-ride, it was back into the circuit again although this time accompanied by a bottle of water and a plentiful supply of paper towels to mop the sweat from my eyes.

It was obvious from the early morning heat, it was already in excess of ninety degrees, that thunderstorms would build in the afternoon and after nearly two hours of flying around the circuit I was ready for a break. The sky was also starting to look fairly ominous with the usual build-up of menacing black clouds. No sooner was I on the ground and the aircraft tied down, than the weather broke bringing with it torrential rain.

After a brief lunch it was back into the flight school to do some more studying for the Meteorology examination which, feeling quietly confident, I took in late afternoon and passed. This now left me with just the Navigation examination to take and of course pass.

I now felt that, at last I seemed to be getting somewhere in my training, all bar one of the examinations successfully completed and I had now flown a further one hour and forty-five minutes solo bringing my total instruction time up to twenty-three hours and twenty minutes and solo time to two hours.

Day twelve dawned bright and clear but I realised that the wind was going to cause major problems today gusting as it was up to twenty knots in the early morning. It was obvious that solo work would only be possible if the wind died down considerably. My instructor decided this was a good day to do some more work on cross wind and short field landings and so we departed up to Winter Haven.

With hindsight, this particular training session was to be a real eye opener in terms of coping with gusting winds although I must admit that flying in these sort of circumstances built up my confidence and left me feeling quite able to cope with the buffeting that the aircraft was receiving. By now, of course, I had mastered the handling technique of thumb and finger on the yoke and rather than fighting to maintain control with large movements of the yoke as I had done previously under the same sort of conditions, it was now delicate touches that were used to keep control of the aircraft. There was no doubt about it, despite all of my initial problems I was definitely learning, and overall my flying was improving.

We did a couple of 'touch-and-go' landings using the whole length of the runway to get used to the gusting wind conditions and then the instructor insisted that I should work on the accuracy of my landings, aiming to land on the runway numbers and on the centreline. This was not an easy exercise at all.

On final approach the wind was doing all that it could to push me to one side of the centreline or the other and with it gusting as it was, it was difficult enough to keep the aircraft in a straight line let alone try and maintain the constant glide-slope down towards the runway necessary for the 'spot' landing. Looking back, this exercise provided me with a fairly steep learning curve in terms of co-ordination of the controls.

Despite the wind conditions, my landings did slowly get closer and closer to the touchdown point defined by the instructor and I have to admit that I did enjoy the challenge. I would also have to admit that I would not have wanted to try the same landings if the instructor had not been sitting beside me!

After lunch the wind had reduced to 13 knots and whilst this was close to the limit of 15 knots that the instructor had set for any solo work, he decided that in the light of the work we had undertaken that morning he was happy to send me off to gain more solo hours towards that magic five-hour figure.

However, after half an hour the winds started to pick up again so it was back down onto the ground for me. In any event, looking back now it was a good day's work with one hour and thirty-five minutes dual instruction and a further thirty-five minutes solo. This now brought my total time up to twenty-seven hours and thirty minutes.

The next day was spent entirely in the circuit at Bartow doing solo work and again there is little for me to reveal to you on this particular aspect apart from the monotony of merely flying round and round the airfield. Again a tip at this point though.

Whilst in the air in the circuit, if you have not done so before, take time to actually gain an appreciation of your surroundings whilst you are looking out for other aircraft. In particular look out for landmarks all around because these will help with the navigation exercises later in your training.

This follows my previous tip of trying to establish early on in your training a picture from the air of all the surrounding countryside that you fly over. Take this mental picture and match it to the charts that you will use later. In other words try and be aware of exactly where you have flown over each day. Do not leave it until the start of the navigation exercises before you look at your charts.

Having completed the two hours and twenty-five minutes to bring me up to the necessary total of five hours solo time, my instructor gave me the details for my first dual cross country which would be made the next day so that I could do the relevant planning in advance. This is where I wish I had had the benefit of my own advice. In my diary entry for the day I wrote

"...at least I should now be able to enjoy Florida from the air. I have not really seen anything of it at all and apart from the good weather I could be anywhere." As I discovered the next day these were to be prophetic words indeed!

At the end of day thirteen of my training I now had a total of thirty hours and twenty five minutes, including that magical figure for solo flying of five hours.

View of the Sebring airfield on approach from the west. The motor racing circuit which also uses one of the old runways can be seen at the bottom.

Day fourteen and my first cross-country was to be relatively short departing from Bartow and flying south east to Sebring, thirty-six nautical miles away. From there I was to go west to Wauchula, a further twenty-nine nautical miles and finally north back to Bartow, another twenty-six nautical miles, making a total round trip of ninety-one nautical miles. Bearing in mind that the intention was merely to find each airfield and over-fly without landing, the whole trip should take just over an hour. Fig. 2.

Having marked the proposed route on the chart with appropriate check points at approximately six to twelve nautical miles between each one along the route, equating to approximately five to ten minutes flying time, and having completed the written flight plan the night before, it was merely a question of phoning for a weather report and calculating the drift off track together with the ground speed, as opposed to the indicated air speed, that would be caused by the prevailing winds. The provision of weather reports is markedly different in the USA from the UK and whilst it is not appropriate to comment on the UK system, it is appropriate to offer some explanation of the service available in the USA.

Pilots in the USA can call the local Flight Service Station (FSS) using a free-phone number which is very easy to remember under the widely-established practice in the USA of using the letters on the key pad to define numbers. By calling 1-800-wx-brief, they can talk to a forecaster to obtain a personalised weather briefing which will include details of the winds at surface level and in the air, cloud conditions, visibility, temperature and altimeter settings.

The briefing also includes details of any Notices to Airmen (NOTAMs) that may affect you. An example would be one giving details of temporary obstructions not to be found on any of the current aeronautical charts and indeed at the time of my training there was one such temporary obstruction, a large construction crane about two miles from the airfield but almost directly on the flight path for one of the runways.

Pilots can also access a computer-based weather-reporting system that contains details of actual conditions at a large number of airfields with weather observation systems. In addition to these, detailed radar and satellite images are available giving a moving picture of the weather as it develops. All in all it is an excellent service provided totally free of charge. Quite apart from all of the above, as you would probably expect in the USA there is also a television channel dedicated entirely to the weather.

Having spoken to the briefer and gained a relatively satisfactory forecast for the trip, that included the prospect of isolated rain showers, it was now merely a question of using the flight computer to calculate the magnetic headings for each stage of the flight taking into account the wind, quoted as being 270 degrees at eight knots, the estimated ground speed together with the distance for each leg and the estimated time of arrival for each check point on the way. Fig. 5 and Fig. 6.

A small tip when flight planning during your training. When marking your chart with the proposed route, having drawn the line from point to point, also draw two parallel lines, one each side of the route, and at a gap from the planned direct route equating to ten nautical miles. In this way, if you do become uncertain of your position, or you miss a check point, because you have originally staged the check points at up to ten nautical miles from each other you can look at the last check point which you identified on the chart and readily distinguish the area that you should now be in having flown no longer than the projected time between check points. This will make life a lot easier for you in the latter stages of your training when the examiner will purposely attempt to get you lost and ask you to identify exactly where you are.

17/6 - DUAL CROSS COUNTRY

WEATHER BRIEF

1-800-WX-BRIEF
(#* THEN *99)

	1st Leg	2nd Leg	3rd Leg
Private Pilot	PHIL STONE		
Type of Aircraft	CESSNA		
Registration	N 66560		
Departure Airfield	BARTON		
Destination	SEBRING	WAUCHULA	BARTOW
Departure Time	11.00		
Flight Duration	70 MINS		
Type of Brief	Standard/Update		

Information as Follows:

Wind:	270 / 8	260 / 7	270/8
Cloud:	BROKEN 2500 SCATTERED 6000	LIFTING TO 3000 SCT 6000	SCT 4000 POSS RAIN
Visibility:	15 + MILES	15 +	REDUCING 10 +
Temperature	29		
Altimeter	3002		

Special Information (NOTAMS etc.)   UNLIT OBSTRUCTION - 300FT - 3 MILES S/E BARTOW

General Information   POSSIBLE RAIN - BECOMING MARGINAL VFR IN AFTERNOON

WIND COULD BECOME VARIABLE 260 / 290 GUSTING 16 KNOTS

Fig 5.

Name __Phil Stone__

Date 21 June   Time of Departure 11.01

Flight details   Navigation Flight Test – Outbound

FROM	TO	MSA	Alt	TAS	TR(T)	W/V	HG(T)	Var	HG(M)	GS	Dist	Time	ETA	ATA	Frequency
WINTER HAVEN	ROAD/LAKE LAKES AF	1400	2000	82	160	030/8	156	4	160	86	10	7	11.08	11.09	122.7 – 122.8
ROAD/LAKE LAKES AF	LAKE BUFFUM	1400	2000	82	160	"	156	4	160	86	8	6	11.15	11.15	122.8
LAKE BUFFUM	AVON PARK AF	1400	2000	82	160	"	156	4	160	86	12	8	11.23	11.23	122.8
AVON PARK AF	SOUTH LAKE/ROAD	1400	2000	82	160	"	156	4	160	86	8	6	11.29	11.30	122.8
SOUTH LAKE/ROAD	PLACID LAKES	1400	2000	82	160	"	156	4	160	86	10	7	11.37	11.38	122.8
PLACID LAKES	ACROSS ROAD	600	2000	82	278	"	283	4	287	85	12	8	11.46		122.8 – 123.0
ACROSS ROAD	RAILWAY + ROAD	600	2000	82	278	"	283	4	287	85	10	7			123.0
RAILWAY + ROAD	MYAKKA CITY	1900	2000	82	278	"	283	4	287	85	18	13			123.0 – 120.1
MYAKKA CITY	ACROSS I-75	1900	2000	82	278	"	283	4	287	85	15	11			120.1
ACROSS I-75	SARASOTA	1900	2000	82	278	"	283	4	287	85	6	4			120.1
	TOTALS										109	77			

DEPARTURE: BARTOW
Ground: 121.9
Tower / CTAF: 121.2
AWOS/ATIS: 133.67 (W.HAVEN)
Runway
Altimeter: 125ft AMSL
Runway Layout: 23 27R 27L 9L 9R 5

EN-ROUTE
FSS: ST PETERSBURG 123.6
Airfield: PLACID LAKES
Airfield: PRIVATE GRASS STRIP
Airfield: RUNWAY 18/36

Fuel Requirements:
Start & Climb: 2
En-route: 13
Circuit & Land: 2
Reserve: 3
TOTAL: 20

Diversion Estimates:
Dest.
HG(M)
Dist.
G/S
ETA

ARRIVAL: SARASOTA
AWOS/ATIS: 134.15
Tower / CTAF: 120.1
Ground: 121.9
Runway
Altimeter: 28ft AMSL
Runway Layout: 22 32 14 4

Fig 6.

61

After completed all the pre-flight planning it was up into the air for my first cross country and a view of what the countryside actually looked like. Much to my surprise the checkpoints on the first leg down to Sebring all appeared on time and in the right place. Another small tip, make sure you choose checkpoints that can be readily identified from the air and do not rely on railway lines as they are sometimes not visible. The checkpoints that I had chosen for this particular leg were Lake Buffum, which by flying along the east shore would ensure that I was on course, a pronounced dog-leg in the Interstate road, 127, and the main road between two airfields, Avon Park and the US Air Force base at Macdill. Both of these airfields have long, easily-identifiable runways and by this stage I knew that I should have sight of Sebring straight ahead.

Whilst it had been the intention to merely over-fly these airfields without landing, as forecast it had started to rain and whilst visibility was still moderate, my instructor decided that we should break early for lunch and let the showers clear before attempting to complete the next two legs of the trip.

Two hours later the weather had cleared so it was off into the air again to fly the next leg across to Wauchula. This leg was slightly more difficult in that there was a real absence of recognisable landmarks once the route had departed from the lakes around Sebring and I had to rely on small roads and rivers, neither of which were easily identifiable from the air. Accurate flying was therefore the key and, roughly on time, the small airfield could be identified straight ahead.

Bearing in mind the unscheduled stop we had made at Sebring my instructor decided to stop at Wauchula and refuel before setting off on the final leg, back up to Bartow. It would also give an opportunity to really test my crosswind landings with the wind being at ninety degrees to the north/south runway. Thankfully the landing was achieved without any problems and after re-fuelling we took off again to return to Bartow.

Whilst again there were relatively few landmarks on the way, there was one, the quarry works at Fort Meade, which could be seen from the air for miles. We were straight on track for this, following which Bartow would be easy to pick out as it was just south east of a large lake, Lake Hancock, and with about ten miles left to go I contacted the Tower at Bartow with the usual prefix of "Good afternoon" for permission to enter the airspace.

The radio work had now really started to improve and when my friendly controller answered my transmission I now knew what to expect him to say. Having written down the details on the pad resting on my kneeboard I could read them back with confidence. He instructed me to report on a left base entry for runway 27 and duly reporting in at the required position and requesting a 'touch-and-go' he cleared us to land.

After the 'touch-and-go', which had merely been to record the actual time of arrival, we set off again to do some instrument work. This was not something that I found particularly enjoyable especially as I had managed to improve on flying by feel rather than fixating on the instruments and having to do this now meant extreme concentration with a constant instrument scan. It was however an important part of the training as it is designed to get you out of trouble in the event of inadvertent entry into cloud.

The essential requirement was to be able to fly a 180-degree turn obviously relying solely on instruments and without any loss of height quite apart from losing control of the aircraft altogether due to disorientation caused by effectively flying 'blind'. It also involved the ability to fly straight and level and be able to climb and descend. The important part of the training was to develop a belief in the instruments rather than necessarily believe what my instincts were telling me.

Returning back to Bartow, my instructor outlined what the following day would involve. This would consist of my first solo cross-country, effectively the same route we had already flown but in reverse. I would fly from Bartow to Wauchula then across to Sebring and back to Bartow. Having at least seen all the landmarks before I should hopefully not get lost! Another three hours of flying meant that my total time was now thirty-three hours and twenty-five minutes.

The next morning, having partially completed the flight plan the day before, all that was necessary now was to phone the weather briefer and input the wind direction and speed to calculate the drift off course together with the estimated speed and timings. The forecast for the day was extremely good with a high level of visibility and light winds from the south which gave me a good deal of reassurance that I was unlikely to get lost on this flight.

Departing from Bartow in the virtually still morning air I set course for Wauchula and could easily make out the quarry works at Fort Meade. The difficult part would be spotting the small airfield from the air although the one thing in my favour was that Wauchula only had one runway facing north to south. In other words it would be straight out in front of me as I approached from the north. Sure enough I could see it in the distance and more surprisingly I was actually on the correct calculated heading and close to the estimated time of arrival. Over-flying the airfield at 2,000 feet I then set course for the next leg to Sebring.

The flight over the same route the previous day had indeed stood me in good stead as whilst there was a general lack of easily-identifiable landmarks I did know that Sebring was just to the north of the large Lake Istokpoga and that I would have to fly along the south shore of Lake Jackson. Even if my flight planning and flying were totally inaccurate, providing I kept a good lookout I should be able to find the airfield. Once again, and perhaps a little bit to my surprise, my flying had been accurate, and there indeed was Sebring Airport in the distance.

Upon calling up to request an airfield advisory over the Sebring Unicom radio frequency, they advised me that the wind was favouring runway 18 and so I duly over flew the airfield and set up for a standard downwind forty-five-degree entry into the circuit. After landing I taxied up to the ramp and parked the aircraft for a refreshment stop. After lunch it was back into the air for the final leg, the return to Bartow. Finding the first two airfields on the cross-country had boosted my confidence no end. Having flown from Bartow so often I now knew what it looked like from the air quite apart from which I knew that providing I kept the small lakes on the way north to the right of me, the relatively large airfield at Bartow would be easily identifiable from a distance, just to the south of Lake Hancock.

And so the second major hurdle on my route to becoming a pilot had now been passed. Not only had I flown solo, but also I had now flown a solo cross-country, and managed to find all the right airfields, at the right time, and without getting lost.

Upon return to Bartow and after a short break to recover, my instructor and I were back in the air to do more instrument work. This was a necessary evil as far as I was concerned as it certainly gets hot with the 'hood' sitting over your head and combined with the intense concentration required seemed to actually make my flying worse, not better.

So at the end of day fifteen, two thirds of the way through the course, my flying times were now twenty nine hours and fifty five minutes of dual instruction and six hours and thirty minutes solo.

Chapter Five

Day Sixteen to Day Twenty-One of the Training

The final week of my training and this was to be where, once again, my confidence was to be severely dented. We had planned a mock Navigation Flight Test that was to be a cross-country flight initially of some 120 nautical miles. After the first leg up to Orlando Country airfield however, and on track for the next destination, Zephyrhills, my instructor would use the dreaded 'hood' to do some instrument flying and try and get me totally lost and confused. Following this I was to establish our position and give diversion estimates in terms of heading and time of arrival back at Bartow.

The flight started well. Bearing in mind that Orlando Country airfield stands just off the north shore of one of the largest lakes in the area, Lake Apopka, and that it is also parallel to a main road that runs alongside it, it was not too difficult to find. As it transpired all of my planning in terms of heading and estimated time of arrival were accurate. After over-flying the airfield I set course for the next airfield, Zephyrhills and this is where things started to go badly wrong.

My instructor took control of the aircraft and whilst I donned the 'hood' he somehow managed without my noticing to turn the direction indicator from the correct setting. This was then my first mistake in not checking the instruments properly and ensuring the direction indicator was correctly aligned with the compass when he handed control of the aircraft back to me.

After approximately ten minutes of flying on what I thought was the correct heading, he told me to remove the 'hood' and tell him exactly where we were. When I looked out of the window I was absolutely horrified to see that we were certainly not where I expected us to be and for some reason I could not match any of the ground references I could see outside with the chart that was on my knees. My mind went a total blank. I thought I recognised a series of masts but when I looked I just could not find them on my chart.

To this day I still have absolutely no idea where I was despite the fact that I cannot have been any more than twenty nautical miles off track. This is where drawing the parallel lines on both sides of my course line on the chart would have been invaluable. At least in my mind it would have substantially narrowed down the area that I must have been in.

Once my instructor had pointed out the differential in the direction indicator and the compass, it was back on with the 'hood' for more instrument flying. After what seemed like an age of flying around on different headings under his instruction, my instructor finally told me to remove the 'hood' again and pointed out Zephyrhills airfield some ten miles ahead where we landed for a review of the lesson so far.

There had understandably been a significant increase in my stress levels at this stage primarily because I was surprised at just how quickly I had become lost. Despite no shortage of lakes and other landmarks around it was just that I could not match them to the chart.

Upon reflection I realise now that I was probably trying to do it the wrong way. Instead of matching what I could actually see from the aircraft to what I could see on the chart I was trying to identify the detail on the chart to the view outside.

After a short break we took off to again try these 'lost' procedures and headed back to Bartow. As before the 'hood' was used after about five minutes into the flight with my instructor getting me to fly around in circles and also at a reduced height of some 700 feet above the ground at which stage he told me to remove the 'hood' and tell him where we were.

This time it should have been a lot easier. The distance between Zephyrhills and Bartow was less than thirty nautical miles and bearing in mind the time we had been flying I knew approximately where we were despite being unable to pinpoint the exact location. In addition to this my estimated heading to enable us to get back to Bartow was obviously inaccurate because after flying in the direction I had indicated for ten or fifteen minutes Bartow should have been straight ahead.

Fortunately I actually spotted the airfield off to the right at about thirty degrees so I had found the field but it was more through luck than by judgement and I knew that was just not good enough. To pass the Navigation Flight Test I had to give the examiner a clear, correct, heading together with estimated time of arrival which needed to be accurate to within a couple of minutes.

Somewhat depressed at this total failure to navigate accurately I landed back at Bartow. I tried to concentrate on studying for the final examination which was Navigation, but my mind was on other matters. I felt that I had achieved so much in the past two weeks but now, yet again, there appeared to be another obstacle that could prove to be insurmountable.

Day sixteen therefore ended on a depressing note. Despite a further three hours and ten minutes instruction on navigation techniques I felt as though I had achieved nothing. Total flying time was now thirty-nine hours and thirty-five minutes.

The next day, day seventeen, the plan of action was to try another mock Navigation Flight Test, this time south-east and down to Avon Park then north-west to Lakeland before returning to Bartow. Just as before the first leg down to Avon Park went without a hitch. The airfield appeared on track, and on time, and whilst this gave me at least some hope that I could navigate correctly, I knew that if I did get lost for any reason I could be hopelessly stuck.

After over-flying Avon Park it was on with the 'hood' although this time my instructor covered up the direction indicator and told me to relax for five minutes whilst he flew the aircraft. I had absolutely no idea where we would be going.

After five minutes the 'hood' came off and control of the aircraft was back in my hands. The surrounding countryside looked extremely familiar but I felt we must have been flying well off the heading that we were supposed to have taken if we were to follow a route to Lakeland. It appeared to me as though we were flying around a series of lakes between Sebring and Lake Wales and it is here where I discovered a neat but simple trick to use if you are ever unsure of the name of a town in Florida.

Most towns in Florida have some sort of tower in the vicinity that nearly always carries the name of the town on its side. Had I known this beforehand it would have made finding my position so much easier because I flew the aircraft over the town and noticed that the name on the side of the tower said "Frostproof" but because it appeared to be next to a large industrial works, and seemed so unlikely for the name of a town, I discounted this as the name of a company.

That was a big mistake. Had I checked the charts properly I would have found that this was indeed the name of a town. So despite all the landmarks available to me in terms of lakes, towers and the name "Frostproof" once again I was convinced that I was lost.

At this point it became obvious to me that whilst I could look out and see all of the available clues as to where we were, I could not assimilate this information in relation to my chart. I could see a lake, but then Florida has thousands of lakes and surely they all look the same from the air? Wrong! Florida lakes are actually quite easy to identify when used with secondary clues.

My instructor pointed out that we had only flown a maximum of ten minutes from Avon Park and so drawing an imaginary circle around that airfield equating to ten minutes flying time, roughly fourteen nautical miles, this must be the area we were in. It was, as he pointed out, a practical impossibility to be anywhere else. There was a large road running along the west shore of one lake and had I looked out of the window properly I would have seen the quarry works at Fort Meade off in the distance to the west. Looking back to my chart I finally found that wonderful name 'Frostproof' and the problem was solved. I had found our position.

This was an easy lesson to learn. Do not make the mistake of concentrating on just the landmarks that appear below you. Look further afield after applying the mental circle to the chart which will give you the area you must be in. This particular lesson was to be my saviour when I undertook the actual Navigation Flight Test as described later. Having established my position it was relatively easy to plot a new course for Lakeland and to give a satisfactory estimate of our time of arrival.

The restaurant at Lakeland is actually located beneath the Control Tower and the accepted request after landing was to 'Taxi to Tony's'. This meant that you quite literally parked and tied down the aircraft right outside the restaurant. After an excellent lunch it was back up into the air for another 'lost' exercise. On went that 'hood' and after twenty minutes of instrument flying off it came again with the standard request of "Tell me where we are?"

This time it was a lot easier. I knew that despite the direction indicator being offset during the instrument flying in order to confuse me, we could not have flown to the west because this would have taken us into the Class B airspace around Tampa and my instructor had not requested clearance to enter their airspace.

On the basis that twenty minutes flying would have taken us roughly thirty nautical miles from Lakeland at the very most, I calculated that if we had been flying in a straight line, which we had not, I could draw the imaginary circle on the chart and that would give me the area we must be in. Using the lesson I had learned previously I could see what appeared to be Zephyrhills airfield in the distance to the west, together with a series of unique shaped lakes up to the north. Whilst there was really nothing readily identifiable beneath us, by using a process of triangulation based on the two identified landmarks I correctly identified that we were over the countryside about fifteen miles north of Winter Haven.

Much to my relief the heading and distance calculation I had given were indeed correct and we duly arrived at Winter Haven to do a touch-and-go to record the actual time before we headed back to Bartow. The weight that seemed to have been lifted from my shoulders was immense. I had finally managed to interpret the landmarks I could see from the air to those that were marked on my chart.

All I had to do now was to repeat the success of this day in the Navigation Flight Test scheduled for the next. With my two hours and forty minutes instruction of today my total flying hours now stood at forty-two hours and fifteen minutes.

First thing the next morning the examiner gave me the route for the Navigation Flight Test telling me that I was to be allowed two hours to do all of the flight planning and to obtain the weather briefing. Figs. 7, 8 & 9. We would fly initially from Bartow to overhead Winter Haven where the test would officially start and then fly south to Placid Lakes, west to Sarasota and finally back to Winter Haven. At least that was the plan.

I already knew that the first leg would be flown to test my accuracy in flight planning. I also knew that whilst we would head initially for Sarasota, we wouldn't actually make it there as this was the leg that the examiner would attempt to get me lost.

The first thing that I did, having marked the route on the chart, was to pick out with a highlighter pen all the possible identifiable landmarks between Placid Lakes and Sarasota in an area of twenty nautical miles either side of track. I realised that after over-flying Placid Lakes there would not be many but felt that the situation did improve after about thirty miles so I hoped that the 'lost' exercise would not happen too early.

The weather forecast was also kind to me. There was absolutely no cloud in the sky, unrestricted visibility and a moderate wind from virtually due north, 030 degrees and eight knots. The only potential problem would be the heat which it was forecast would bring in thunderstorms in the late afternoon.

In late morning we duly set off from Bartow and flew up to Winter Haven where the test would begin. I had flown part of the route to Placid Lakes many times before and knew this would take us down past Lakes Wales airfield, past my now favourite town of Frostproof, virtually straight over Avon Park airfield and then alongside a series of lakes leading down to the airfield at Placid Lakes. I had no idea what this airfield looked like although I did know that it was a private grass strip.

On the way down my course headings and timings for each check point were accurate and on this basis, even if the airfield was difficult to spot from the air, it should appear straight ahead just before the estimated time of arrival. It did. It was also a good job that it did. It was no more than a small grass airfield with one hangar and no signs of any aircraft on the ground. At least the first part of the test had been successful but this was where the real fun would start.

Once we were directly overhead of Placid Lakes airfield I set course for Sarasota and it was at this point where the 'hood' came out in addition to which the examiner instructed me to reduce altitude to 700 feet. I had a sneaky feeling that the examiner would pull the same stunt as my instructor and alter the direction indicator whilst I was distracted. I also knew that whilst he was giving me that part of the test which relates to flying on instruments I could not rely on this for information as to which direction we were actually flying in.

The control tower at Lakeland - Tony's restaurant is on the left and the photograph was taken from where we parked the aircraft.

As it transpired I was right. Having removed the 'hood' I checked the direction indicator to the compass, found it to be inaccurate, and reset it. Now was the time to find where we were.

In order to not only buy myself some time but also to improve the area of countryside over which I could see, I applied full power and went back up to 2,000 feet in a series of climbing turns whilst at the same time looking for those all-important landmarks.

Just for once there was actually a railway line running north to south with a relatively large town to the south about ten miles away and what appeared to be a race track some five miles away. On looking in the opposite direction this was where I appreciated that the lesson about looking into the distance came into its own. I could see an airfield to the north, with one north to south runway and that confirmed my position. The large town was Arcadia, the runway was at Wauchula and I was halfway between the two at a little place called Limestone.

Having established my position the next thing to do was to give the examiner a heading and estimated time of arrival for a diversion airfield. In this case it was to be back to Bartow. This was where I was extremely grateful for the moderate prevailing wind. As it had been correctly forecast as being from virtually due north I knew this would not cause any great drift from the heading and hopefully would not cause too many problems with the timing.

Using the rule of thumb, a neat little trick which means that having measured the width of your thumb you know how many nautical miles it equates too, in my case seven, I estimated the distance as thirty-eight nautical miles. The estimated time of arrival would therefore be thirty minutes and we would fly on a magnetic heading of 010 degrees. Exactly thirty-one minutes later we were on the ground with the examiner confirming that I had passed the test.

21/6 — NAVIGATION FLIGHT TEST.

WEATHER BRIEF

1-800-WX-BRIEF
(#* THEN *99)

	1st Leg	2nd Leg	3rd Leg
Private Pilot	PHIL STONE		
Type of Aircraft	CESSNA		
Registration	N 66560		
Departure Airfield	BARTOW		
Destination	PLACID LAKES	SARASOTA	BARTOW
Departure Time	11.00		
Flight Duration	140 MINS		
Type of Brief	Standard/~~Update~~		

Information as Follows:

Wind:	040/8	020/8	040/8
Cloud:	CLEAR	CLEAR	CLEAR
Visibility	20+ MILES	20+ MILES	20+ MILES
Temperature	28	29	30+ LATE P.M.
Altimeter	3010	3011	3010

Special Information (NOTAMS etc.)

CRANE - 3M S/E BARTOW

MOORED BALLOON TO 250 FT - 5M NORTH - SARASOTA

General Information

GOOD HIGH PRESSURE OVER WEST COAST

POSSIBLE SCATTERED THUNDERSTORMS AFTER 3PM

Fig 7.

Name **PHIL STONE**

Date **21 JUNE** Flight details **NAVIGATION FLIGHT TEST – RETURN** Time of Departure _____

FROM	TO	MSA	Alt	TAS	TR(T)	W/V	HG(T)	Var	HG(M)	GS	Dist	Time	ETA	ATA	Frequency
SARASOTA	ACROSS I75	1800	2000	82	051	030/8	049	4	053	75	6	5			121.9 – 120.1
I75	2ND ROAD	1800	2000	82	051	"	049	4	053	75	8	6			120.1 – 122.7
2ND ROAD	LH MAST (649)	1800	2000	82	051	"	049	4	053	75	15	12			122.7 – 121.2
MAST	MINE/RAILWAY	1800	2000	82	051	"	049	4	053	75	18	14			121.2
MINE/RAILWAY	BARTOW	1800	2000	82	051	"	049	4	053	75	10	8			121.2 – 121.9
DIVERSION															
LIMESTONE	BARTOW	1800	2000	82	005	030/8	006	4	010	75	38	30	12.46	12.47	
										TOTALS	57	45			

EN-ROUTE	
FSS	ST PETERSBURG 123.6
Airfield	
Airfield	
Airfield	
Airfield	

Fuel Requirements	
Start & Climb	2
En-route	13
Circuit & Land	2
Reserve	3
TOTAL	20

DEPARTURE	SARASOTA
Ground / CTAF	121.9
Tower / CTAF	120.1
AWOS / ATIS	134.15
Runway	
Altimeter	28 ft AMSL
Runway Layout	

(Runway Layout diagram: 14 / 22 / 4 / 32)

Diversion Estimates	
Dest.	BARTOW
HG(M)	010
Dist.	38
G/S	75
ETA	30 MINS

ARRIVAL	BARTOW
AWOS / ATIS	
Tower / CTAF	121.2
Ground	121.9
Runway	
Altimeter	125 ft AMSL
Runway Layout	

(Runway Layout diagram: 9L / 9R / 27R / 27L / 23 / 5)

Fig 8.

Name __Phil Stone__

Date 22 June   Time of Departure 12.15

Flight details __Qualifying Solo Cross Country - Outbound__

FROM	TO	MSA	Alt	TAS	TR(T)	W/V	HG(T)	Var	HG(M)	GS	Dist	Time	ETA	ATA	Frequency
WINTER HAVEN	CROSS I4	1300	2000	82	340	005/4	341	4	345	78	6	5	12.20	12.20	22.7
CROSS I4	EVA-ACROSS ROAD	1300	2000	82	340	=	341	"	345	78	10	8	12.28	12.29	22.7
EVA ACROSS ROAD	LAKE KLINGER	1300	2000	82	340	"	341	"	345	78	8	8	12.37	12.38	122.7 - 122.8
LAKE KLINGER	RAILWAY/ROAD	900	2000	82	340	"	341	"	345	78	14	11	12.43	12.43	122.8 - 122.7
RAILWAY/ROAD	COLEMAN/ROAD	900	2000	82	340	"	341	"	345	78	14	11	12.54	12.56	122.7
COLEMAN/ROAD	ITS + MAST (480)	900	2000	82	340	"	341	"	345	78	9	7	13.03	13.04	122.7 - 123.0
ITS + MAST	ITS + RACETRACK	1600	2000	82	340	"	341	"	345	78	6	5	13.09	13.09	123.0
ITS + RACETRACK	OCALA-TAYLOR	1600	2000	82	340	"	341	"	345	78	10	8	13.17	13.18	123.0

TOTALS   72   57

DEPARTURE WINTER HAVEN

Ground	
Tower / CTAF	122.7
AWOS / ATIS	133.67
Runway	
Altimeter	146 ft AMSL

Runway Layout

11   4   22   29

EN-ROUTE

FSS	
Airfield	ST PETERSBURG 123.6
Airfield	BARTOW TO WINTER HAVEN - 121.2
Airfield	BARTOW (PLANT) - 122.8
Airfield	LEESBURG - 122.7

ARRIVAL OCALA-TAYLOR

AWOS/ATIS	128.125
Tower / CTAF	123.0
Ground	
Runway	
Altimeter	90 ft AMSL

Runway Layout

8   26   18   36

Fuel Requirements		Diversion Estimates	
Start & Climb	2	Dest.	
En-route	12	HG(M)	
Circuit & Land	2	Dist.	
Reserve	3	G/S	
TOTAL	19	ETA	

Fig 9.

The relief that I felt after all the previous trials and tribulations in the practice tests was tremendous. I now only had three more hurdles to overcome before achieving that coveted Private Pilot's Licence. There was the last remaining written exam, Navigation, the solo qualifying cross-country flight scheduled for the next day and then the final General Flight Test.

I was now beginning to feel that I could finally succeed. Total flying time on this the eighteenth day of training amounted to two hours and ten minutes bringing the total time up to forty-four hours and twenty-five minutes including solo time now of eight hours and forty minutes.

Following on from the success of the previous day it was now time to really prove that I could navigate. The qualifying solo cross-country would be the longest flight I had attempted on my own so far, a total of some one hundred and fifty nautical miles. In order to prove that I had actually flown the route I had to obtain a signature at each airfield.

The route was to be Bartow to Winter Haven then north up to Ocala-Taylor, back south to Zephyrhills before over-flying Winter Haven to complete the timings and then return to Bartow. Figs 10, 11 & 12.

Obtaining a weather brief revealed that the forecast was very similar to that of the previous day. Totally clear skies with visibility in excess of fifteen miles and light winds from the north, 005 degrees at four knots. The only potential problem for this flight seemed to be a warning from the weather briefer that there would be substantial sky-diving activity over Zephyrhills and there were likely to be thunderstorms in the late afternoon.

The flight plan took me some time to complete and after it had been checked by my instructor it was actually midday when I departed from Bartow. I flew up to Winter Haven to start the official timing for the route and set course for the first leg of the cross-country up to Ocala-Taylor airfield. Despite the light winds there was still a substantial number of thermals in the air and the aircraft was bouncing around all over the place.

Once again however all my planning proved accurate and in just over an hour Ocala-Taylor airfield appeared straight ahead. I had been advised by my instructor to use the phrase "student pilot on qualifying cross-country" when calling up the airfield for traffic information and this prompted a surprise response.

After landing and taxiing to the ramp I was met by a marshaller who directed me to where the aircraft should be parked. He chocked the wheels and gave me a lift in his buggy up to the administration building to get the required signature from the airport manager. I realised then that this sort of reception was obviously in response to my initial radio call.

All the other airfields I had visited during the course of my training had effectively left me to decide for myself where to park the aircraft. In my case it was normally as close as possible to the administration building to reduce the length of the walk. After stopping in the airfield cafÈ to have something to eat it was time to get back in the air and try and find Zephyrhills.

I felt that this should not present any problem as I had actually flown into Zephyrhills before and therefore knew what it looked like from the air. The only worry for me of course was the potential sky-divers and as I listened out on the radio my worst fears were confirmed. I was on track and on time, being about twenty minutes out from Zephyrhills, as I heard the jump plane giving the standard warnings to all traffic in the air that sky-diving would commence in fifteen minutes.

This would mean that the sky-divers would be in the air and floating down to earth just as I would be making my approach. I decided therefore that the best thing to do would be to delay my arrival by at least ten minutes. Once I had the airfield in sight I

Ocala-Taylor airfield taken on approach from the south-east.

flew around in a wide circle until both the jump plane and the sky-divers were on the ground before making the standard radio call advising of my intention to join the circuit for a full stop landing using of course the magic words 'student pilot on qualifying cross-country'.

After joining the circuit I duly landed. This time I was directed over the radio by the airport manager to bring the aircraft up and park right outside the administration building. More red carpet treatment! I obtained the obligatory signature to prove that I had

22/6 — SOLO QUALIFYING CROSS COUNTRY.

WEATHER BRIEF

1-800-WX-BRIEF
(#* THEN *99)

	1st Leg	2nd Leg	3rd Leg
Private Pilot	PHIL STONE		
Type of Aircraft	CESSNA		
Registration	N 66560		
Departure Airfield	WINTER HAVEN	OCALA - TAYLOR	ZEPHYRHILLS
Destination	OCALA - TAYLOR	ZEPHYRHILLS	BARTOW
Departure Time	12.00	14.00	15.15
Flight Duration	4 HRS - WITH STOPS		
Type of Brief	Standard/Update		

Information as Follows:

Wind:	005 / 4	010 / 3	010 / 4
Cloud:	CLEAR	CLEAR	CLEAR
Visibility	15+ MILES	20+ MILES	20+ MILES
Temperature	28	30	30
Altimeter	3011	3010	3011

Special Information
(NOTAMS etc.)   CRANE - 3 MILES S/E BARTOW . 300 FT

General Information   SIGNIFICANT SKY-DIVING AT ZEPHYRHILLS ALL DAY

POSSIBLE THUNDERSTORMS AFTER 4 PM

HIGH PRESSURE OVER CENTRAL FLORIDA - MOVING SLOWLY EAST

Fig. 10.

Name: PHIL STONE

Date: 22 JUNE   Time of Departure: 12.15

Flight details: QUALIFYING SOLO Cross Country - OUTBOUND

FROM	TO	MSA	Alt	TAS	TR(T)	W/V	HG(T)	Var	HG(M)	GS	Dist	Time	ETA	ATA	Frequency
WINTER HAVEN	CROSS I-4	1300	2000	82	340	005/4	341	4	345	78	6	5	12.20	12.20	122.7
CROSS I-4	EVA-ACROSS ROAD	1300	2000	82	340	"	341	"	345	72	10	8	12.28	12.29	122.7
EVA ACROSS ROAD	LAKE KLINGER	1300	2000	82	340	"	341	"	345	78	11	8	12.37	12.38	122.7 – 122.8
LAKE KLINGER	RAILWAY/ROAD	900	2000	82	340	"	341	"	345	78	6	5	12.43	12.43	122.8 – 122.7
RAILWAY/ROAD	COLEMAN/ROAD	900	2000	82	340	"	341	"	345	78	14	11	12.54	12.56	122.7
COLEMAN/ROAD	ITS + MAST (480)	900	2000	82	340	"	341	"	345	78	9	7	13.03	13.04	122.7 – 123.0
ITS + MAST	ITS + RAILTRACK	1600	2000	82	340	"	341	"	345	78	6	5	13.09	13.09	123.0
ITS + RAILTRACK	OCALA-TAYLOR	1600	2000	82	340	"	341	"	345	78	10	8	13.17	13.18	123.0

TOTALS: 72   57

EN-ROUTE

FSS	ST PETERSBURG 123.6
Airfield	BARTOW TO WINTER HAVEN – 121.2
Airfield	BRODAIR (PRIVATE) – 122.8
Airfield	LEESBURG – 122.7
Airfield	

Fuel Requirements

Start & Climb	2
En-route	12
Circuit & Land	2
Reserve	3
TOTAL	19

Diversion Estimates

Dest.
HG(M)
Dist.
G/S
ETA

DEPARTURE

DEPARTURE	WINTER HAVEN
Ground	
Tower / CTAF	122.7
AWOS / ATIS	133.67
Runway	
Altimeter	146 ft AMSL
Runway Layout	

Runway Layout: 11 / 22 / 29 / 4

ARRIVAL

ARRIVAL	OCALA-TAYLOR
AWOS / ATIS	128.125
Tower / CTAF	123.0
Ground	
Runway	
Altimeter	90 ft AMSL
Runway Layout	

Runway Layout: 18 / 36 / 8 / 26

Fig. 11.

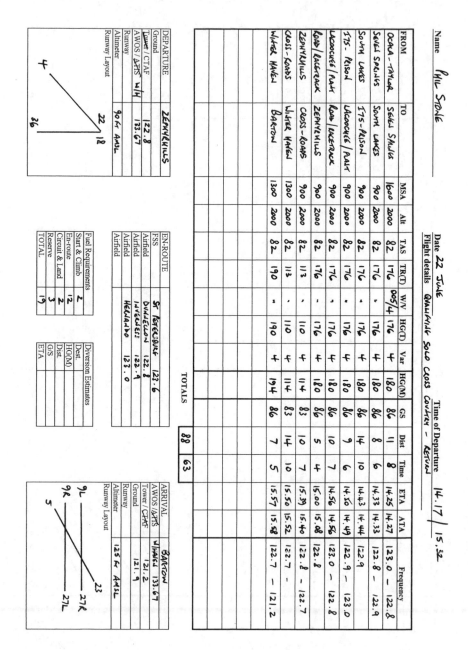

Fig. 12.

actually landed at Zephyrhills following which it was off and back to Winter Haven. This was to be a relatively short hop after the last two legs, to complete the timings for the flight plan and then a final return to Bartow.

Obviously for me this was the high point of my training. I had managed to fly a round trip in excess of 150 nautical miles on time, without any problems and more importantly, without getting lost. Solo time for the day was three hours and ten minutes giving me total time of forty-seven hours thirty-five minutes.

With two days left of the course the next day was to be spent on preparation for the General Flight Test where I would have to demonstrate various landings and take-offs, together with practice forced landings to test my ability in the event of engine failure. I was confident that I could perform these without difficulty but I knew that I still needed more practice on stalls and incipient spins.

I also, for the first time, had to get some practice on steep level turns as well as on recovering the aircraft to straight and level flight after it had been put into an unusual attitude by my instructor. This was where he would get me to close my eyes whilst he flew the plane up, down and all over to disorientate me and then hand control back to me after placing the aircraft into a steep climb or dive. I was also still somewhat dubious about those stalls, especially when the wing dropped and causing a partial spin entry. My reservations about these exercises showed in the quality of my flying that morning.

My instructor and I initially flew up to Winter Haven to practise the required landings and take-offs in a number of different aircraft configurations. These had to be with and without flaps, glide approaches, go-arounds, short field and soft field landings. All of these went well and remembering the early problems I had with landings at the start of my training I was greatly encouraged. It was however a different story with the practice stalls.

For some reason I was experiencing great difficulty in keeping the wings level just prior to the stall. Each time this happened the aircraft would break away into an incipient spin and whilst I could, by now, recover control it should not have been happening.

There still also remained the question of those unusual attitudes and also the steep level turns neither of which we had tried before. Bearing in mind the early experience I had with the stall which had frightened the life out me, I asked my instructor to demonstrate the unusual attitude recovery first of all and it was not as bad as I had expected.

He demonstrated two basic forms of unusual attitude. The first was with the aircraft climbing with reducing airspeed and the second with the aircraft diving with increasing airspeed. Whilst I was initially disorientated it was relatively easy to recover from each of these into straight and level flight. The steep level turns were however a different matter. The idea was to turn the aircraft through 360 degrees in as tight a circle as possible which, if achieved, meant that we should pass through our own wake turbulence caused by the propeller. What the instructor neglected to tell me was that in a 60-degree banked turn we would be pulling at least 2g or in other words we would feel as though we were twice our actual body weight.

This was an extremely unpleasant experience. I had never flown in such a violent fashion before with the aircraft appearing to fly almost on its side. The view out of the side window appeared to be almost vertical to the ground although with the extra force of gravity I was actually pinned to my seat. Nevertheless I still had to master the exercise and I had no intention of failing now. The greatest problem for me was actually applying sufficient bank of the wings to make the turn steep enough although after a number of attempts we did finally manage to pass through our own wake.

At this stage unfortunately the weather started to deteriorate and whilst the usual thunderstorms were not forecast until the afternoon it was obviously time to get back onto the ground. As it transpired this was probably a mixed blessing for whilst we had a lot of final brushing up to do on my flying I still had the written Navigation exam left to sit. After several hours of revision the exam was successfully passed in the afternoon.

This left just one more hurdle, the General Flight Test, and that was scheduled for the next day, which was the final full day of the course. Despite the early break due to the weather I had still flown for two hours and thirty-five minutes that day giving me a total flying time now of fifty hours and ten minutes.

Cessna 150 registration N66560 - taken at Ocala-Taylor on solo-qualifying cross-country

As the final day, day twenty-one, dawned I realised that I still had a lot to do. The General Flight Test was scheduled for the early afternoon so first thing in the morning it was into the air to try and sort out those steep turns and stalls. My instructor and I departed in the usual Cessna 150, N66560, but on climbing away from the runway, the tower controller reported signs of smoke coming from the aircraft.

I immediately completed an extremely tight circuit ready to get back down on the ground when the controller reported that he could have been mistaken as there was no further sign of smoke. He suggested a low level pass down the runway so that he could take a better look and this was what we did, flying the aircraft down the runway at the same height as the tower. The controller confirmed no further sign of any smoke, but as we applied full power and climbed away, he changed his mind and again reported smoke.

Time to get on the ground, and fast. I completed another tight circuit, remaining within glide distance of all three runways and landed without any problem.

This mechanical problem did however pose a new problem for me. The vast majority of my training had been undertaken in this one aircraft, in which I felt comfortable, but now I was going to be forced to fly a different aircraft for the General Flight Test. As it transpired I had no need to worry.

Changing to a different Cessna 150, registration N19BS, we took off and flew up to Winter Haven to do some practice landings. Following these we flew off to the practice area over the open countryside north of Winter Haven to get back into those stalls and steep turns. For some inexplicable reason this aircraft handled totally different in the stall but this was to be to my advantage.

Instead of the wing dropping each time which placed us into an incipient spin, the aircraft remained totally balanced. Right up to the stall the wings remained level and instead of a sharp break earthwards the nose seemed to just bob gently down making recovery simple. Perhaps the original aircraft, N66560, had taken a dislike to me after all those bad landings!

After some two and a half hours in the air I was feeling completely confident and ready for the test. It was early afternoon when I took off again with the examiner. This was to be the final hurdle to my licence, the General Flight Test. Prior to the test the examiner had briefed me on what to expect and had gone over the rough order in which we would go through the relevant exercises. That was of course all except for the practice forced landing which he warned me could come at any time. We would start off with the stalls and steep turns and then proceed into the various landing and take-off configurations.

I was quite pleased that we started with the stalls for I knew that if they went badly at the beginning of the test we could perhaps try them again at the end. I had no need to worry. The aircraft handled beautifully just as it had done in the morning and after demonstrating four stalls in different configurations, with and without power and with and without flaps the examiner was duly satisfied.

This was a good start. Next we went into the steep turns. The examiner was not immediately satisfied with these for he felt that they were just not steep enough and he then demonstrated exactly what it was he wanted to see. If I had believed that the steep turns practised previously with my instructor were steep then I had seen nothing. The turn that the examiner demonstrated appeared to make the aircraft actually fly around its own wingtip putting us seemingly at ninety degrees to the ground. Then it was my turn.

It did not seem anywhere near as steep, certainly steeper than my original attempts but not as steep as the examiner had just demonstrated. To my surprise and relief however we did pass through our own wake turbulence and this satisfied the examiner. So with all the upper air exercises completed it was back to Winter Haven to complete the various landings.

I should have known better than to relax. With Winter Haven airfield in sight, the examiner pulled the power off for a simulated engine failure. Decision time. Was I close enough to glide in to the airfield or was it time to pick a suitable field? I decided that we would never make any of the runways and selected what appeared to be a fairly long field. As it transpired that was the correct decision.

The examiner had purposely pulled the power here because if I had chosen to try and glide in we would never have made it to the airfield. Setting the aircraft up for landing we gradually drew closer and closer to the ground. Still with the power off I began to wonder whether the examiner actually intended landing in this field. Further down we went until at last the instruction came for me to apply full power and climb out. Another part of the test satisfactorily completed.

Into Winter Haven airfield then for the final part of the test, landings and take-offs. I had to demonstrate various landing configurations including with and without flaps, soft field and short field and cross-wind. For the final cross-wind landing we actually changed runways so that we could use one that was not favoured by the prevailing wind. This would increase the cross-wind component or that was what I thought.

In actual fact the change of runway was to ensure that immediately after completing the touch and go we would fly directly over a lake. No sooner had we taken off, at a couple of hundred feet above the ground, the examiner again pulled the power off for a simulated engine failure and asked where I was going to land now. No choice whatsoever, it would have to be in the lake! I knew that the examiner was testing to see whether I would attempt the so-called impossible turn, and attempt to land on the runway that we taken off from. No chance!

As I applied full power again to recover and climb away, the examiner seemed satisfied and I understandably hoped that I had done well enough to gain a pass. We flew back to Bartow and after landing and parking the aircraft the examiner merely opened the door and just walked away without a word.

Had I passed? The answer was yes. I could not believe it. After all the trials and tribulations of the past three weeks I had actually done it. I was now a Private Pilot. It had taken me a total of fifty-four hours and fifty-five minutes, but I had done it!

Chapter Six

The Return to the UK

Upon my return to the UK I knew that I would be flying Piper Warriors at Newcastle and therefore before leaving Florida I wanted to at least gain some experience of flying this different aircraft. I accordingly arranged with the school's owner to have an hours flying in a Warrior for the morning of my last day in Florida.

He went through the full pre-flight check routine and briefed me on the differences between the Cessna 150 and the Piper Warrior and then we took off for Lake Wales airfield to carry out some practice landings. After all the problems I had initially encountered in landing the Cessna, the Warrior was totally different. It was relatively easy to land in addition to which, being a four-seater, I actually had room in the cockpit unlike the confines of the two-seater Cessna where we were literally squashed together.

The whole flight went very well and hopefully this would place me in good stead for the check-ride that I would have to undertake upon my return to Newcastle. Later that same day saw me at Orlando airport for the overnight return flight to Gatwick and then on to Newcastle.

For the next four weeks there was nothing I could do except wait for my new Private Pilot Licence to come from Flight Crew Licensing at the Civil Aviation Authority. When it did finally arrive I telephoned the Aero club at Newcastle and booked a flight with its Chief Flying Instructor.

This was an extremely apprehensive time for me. I had gained the licence but could I now satisfy the Aero club that I could fly sufficiently well to enable me to hire its aircraft? The day of the check-ride arrived and I drove to the airport with some trepidation.

The instructor examined my flying logbook, medical certificate and licence and then accompanied me out to the aircraft to watch me make the pre-flight checks. Once completed we climbed into the cockpit, completed the internal checks and then contacted the tower for taxi instructions. After the problems I had initially encountered with the tower controller at Bartow, Newcastle tower was a completely different story. The speed of communication was more measured and with the Aero club positioned as it is at the end of the runway there is only one hold point to taxi to.

Depending on the wind direction, and bearing in mind the single runway, there are also only two options for take-off direction. You either enter the runway from the hold and take-off to the east or backtrack down the runway, turn the aircraft around and take-off to the west. Once we had completed all the final checks we were given our take-off clearance and we departed up to the north and the open countryside of Northumberland.

This flight was actually to turn into the equivalent of a full General Flight Test. The instructor wanted me to demonstrate a full range of stalls together with steep turns and other general handling exercises. All of these passed without problem and so we returned to the airport so that I could demonstrate landing in different configurations. Again these went without a hitch and the instructor confirmed that subject to a further hour flying purely in the circuit to get used to the instructions of air traffic control he was happy for me to hire their aircraft.

He explained the reason for the further hour was that bearing in mind Newcastle is a busy airport used by numerous large jets I would have to get used to various holding procedures. Obviously the commercial aircraft have priority and therefore it was often necessary to fly holding patterns to make way for them when landing or taking off.

As it transpired this experience was absolutely vital. I had learnt to fly at small airfields and had no experience of sharing the airspace with large commercial jets. A week later I was back at the airport to complete this final hour of the check-ride. This time I was to be accompanied by a different instructor who was only really there to offer me guidance if any problems occurred in the circuit.

Despite numerous interruptions to our circuit work to allow the commercial jets priority everything went smoothly and I was duly signed off to hire and fly their aircraft. This had removed my greatest fear. It was all very well to gain the licence in Florida but unless I could use it in the UK from Newcastle it would be of little use to me. I could now go out and really enjoy my flying. My ambition had been achieved.

The author with the Piper Warrior PA28-15 1 registration N32401 used on the final day to gain experience ready for the return to the UK. The author now has over 160 hours logged flying this aircraft type.